Breakthroughs in Commodity Technical Analysis

BREAKTHROUGHS IN COMMODITY

TECHNICAL ANALYSIS

By J. D. Hamon

Windsor Books, Brightwaters, New York

Published by Windsor Books
P. O. Box 280
Brightwaters, N. Y., 11718

Manufactured in the United States of America

ISBN 0-930233-01-8

Acknowledgement

I would like to express appreciation to the floor traders, research analysts, and traders who have given me tips, comments and suggestions.

J. D. Hamon

Table Of Contents

Illustrations

Introduction

After finishing my second book I did not intend to reveal any more trading techniques; but pressure from friends has caused me to change my mind. I also decided to give more explicit detail for putting on trades. This ought to give most traders the information needed to make money in the market.

To the many who have written or phoned saying they have made good profits after reading my work, this may not seem urgent; but some have asked for more help. As I told one person, however, you do not learn to trade by merely reading a book. The trader must test a system until he knows why and how it all fits together. The beginner in particular needs to do a lot of experimenting and evaluating. This book will offer every trader, from beginner to expert, additional knowledge on technical commodity trading.

Everyone must develop his own style. No one can do this for you unless he is a full time coach. If you want a simple, easy way to be in the market, then let an account manager do the trading. It takes work to learn to trade. I hope I've made things a lot easier with my computer programs and books, but acquiring the skill is a matter of practice and work.

Chapter One

Balance Point Line Extensions

INTRODUCTION—
USING BALANCE POINT LINE EXTENSIONS

You can be one of the few people to know how to predict how far the next swing will go with an 80% accuracy. Testing of trades using only the BPL's showed them to be 80% accurate on a per trade basis. Profit totals would have been fantastic if I had totaled the money won. It is hard to get this good a win/loss ratio on a per trade basis, unless the method is exceptionally accurate.

HOW YOU CAN USE BALANCE POINT LINES

Keep charts of the commodities you like to follow. It did not matter which commodities were used, as there were good results on all of them. My first book, **"Advanced Commodity Trading Techniques"** explained how to make BPL's. However, I did not make a point of extending the lines out beyond the current day's price to predict where the next resistance level would be.

A Balance Point Line is made by drawing a line through the mid-points or centers of two or more swings. The line must be straight, but may be in any direction and can be of any length as long as the centers of several swings are connected. It has no definite place of origin and is not restricted to consecutive swings. Usually better results are obtained if the last swing is bisected, but this does not always hold true (see Figure 1).

15

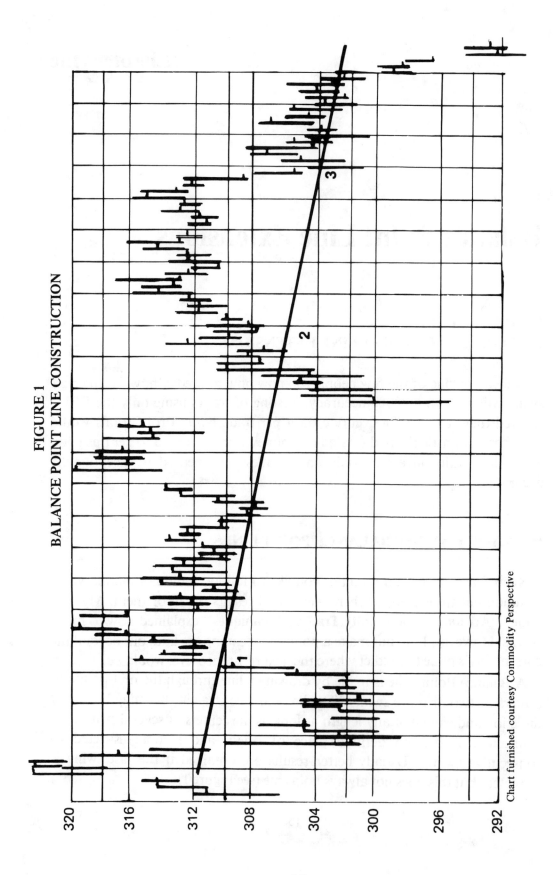

FIGURE 1
BALANCE POINT LINE CONSTRUCTION

Chart furnished courtesy Commodity Perspective

16

There are numerous examples in Figures 2-7. In most of the examples price stopped at the line. But in a runaway market, price would go on through the BPL line and travel the same distance beyond its intersection of the BPL. All one need do is trade when it goes through the lines knowing that there is a good chance it would go the same distance beyond as it travelled before reaching the line. All that's required is to draw a line through the last two swings, then extend this line out so it will intercept price. If price has already gone through the line, you can tell how much further it should travel. Just draw a line through the center of the last two swings.

When the price pattern starts getting into a channel the line will be in the middle. Here you must trade from the outer edges. With tight choppy markets trade from the channel highs and lows.

Occasionally there will not be two consecutive swings in position for a line through them to extend into price action. You can skip back one swing if necessary, as missing a swing will not hurt. The BPL lines do not have to go through the last two swings in succession. They can be through the middle of one, then skip one and catch the last one. Most of the time this will find a pivot. If it does not, price usually will go the same distance on the other side. If a narrow channel appears, you skip a swing as these do not usually help find the next pivot.

MISSING A GOOD THING

Many readers of my first book did not understand the significance of what can be done with BPL's. I did not reveal how to extend the lines; but those traders who worked with them learned and have told me that this has been very successful. This explanation is to make sure everyone understands the potential uses of these lines.

SUCCESSFUL SINCE 1978

I have been using these lines since 1978, and have found them reliable. They were recently tested over back price charts. There were usually about ten or twelve trades per page of each commodity. Never did I find more

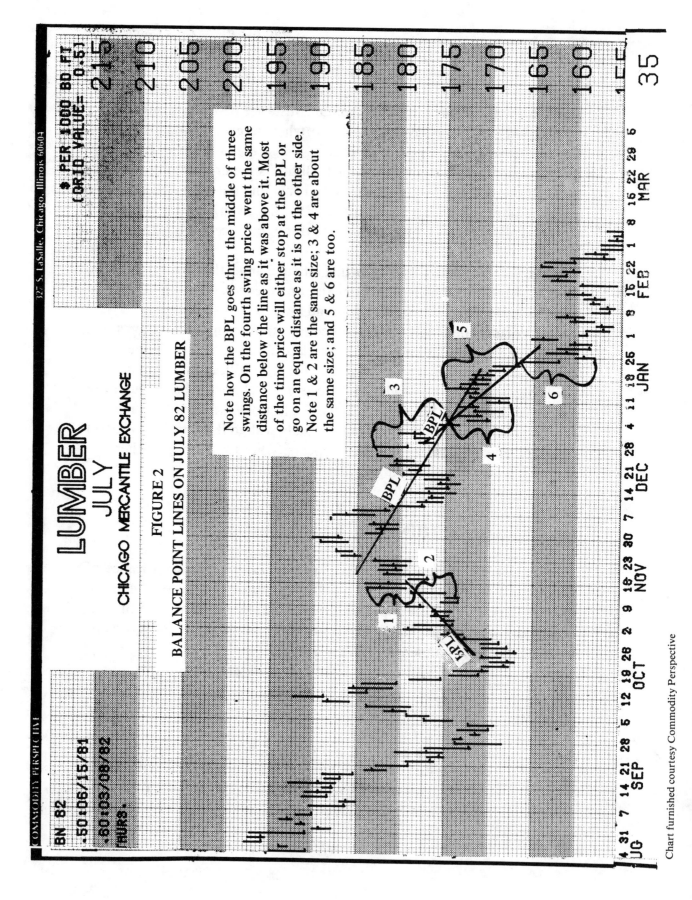

LUMBER

JULY

CHICAGO MERCANTILE EXCHANGE

FIGURE 2

BALANCE POINT LINES ON JULY 82 LUMBER

Note how the BPL goes thru the middle of three swings. On the fourth swing price went the same distance below the line as it was above it. Most of the time price will either stop at the BPL or go on an equal distance as it is on the other side. Note 1 & 2 are the same size; 3 & 4 are about the same size; and 5 & 6 are too.

18

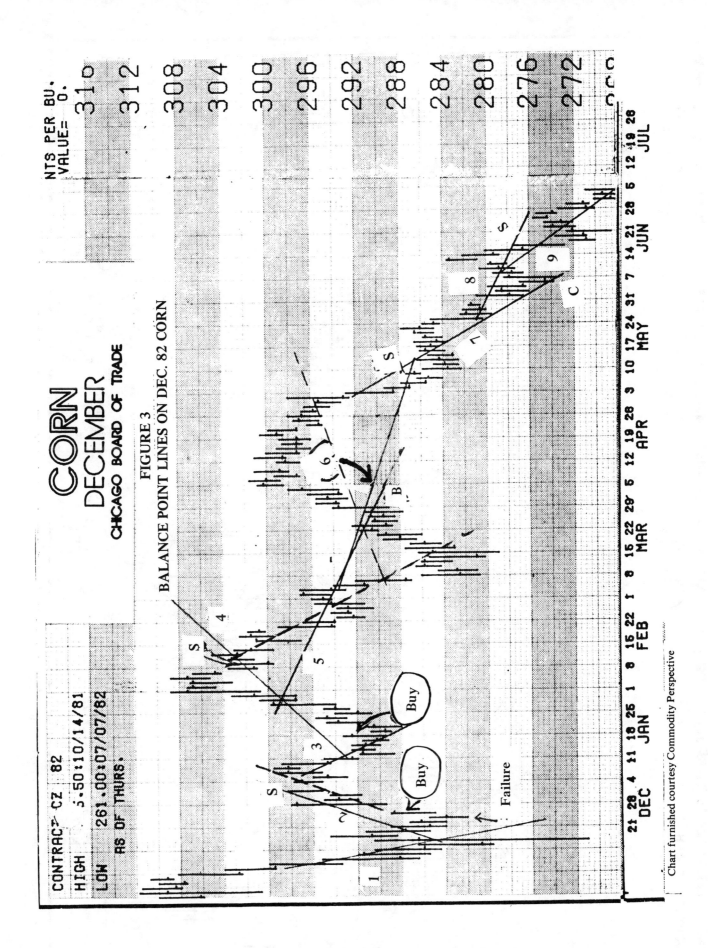

CORN
DECEMBER
CHICAGO BOARD OF TRADE

FIGURE 3
BALANCE POINT LINES ON DEC. 82 CORN

Chart furnished courtesy Commodity Perspective

19

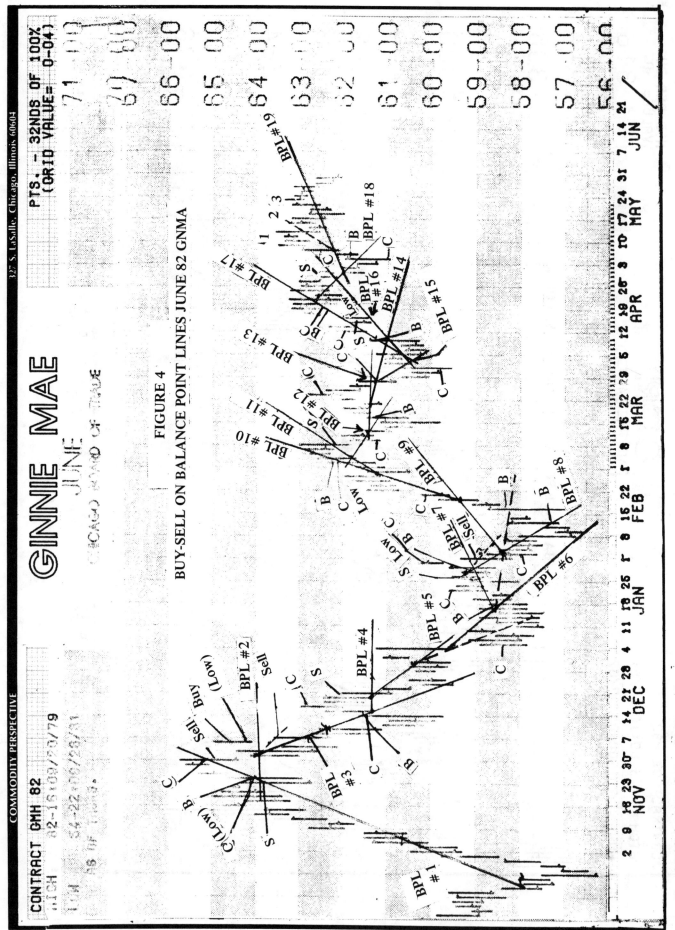

FIGURE 4

BUY-SELL ON BALANCE POINT LINES JUNE 82 GNMA

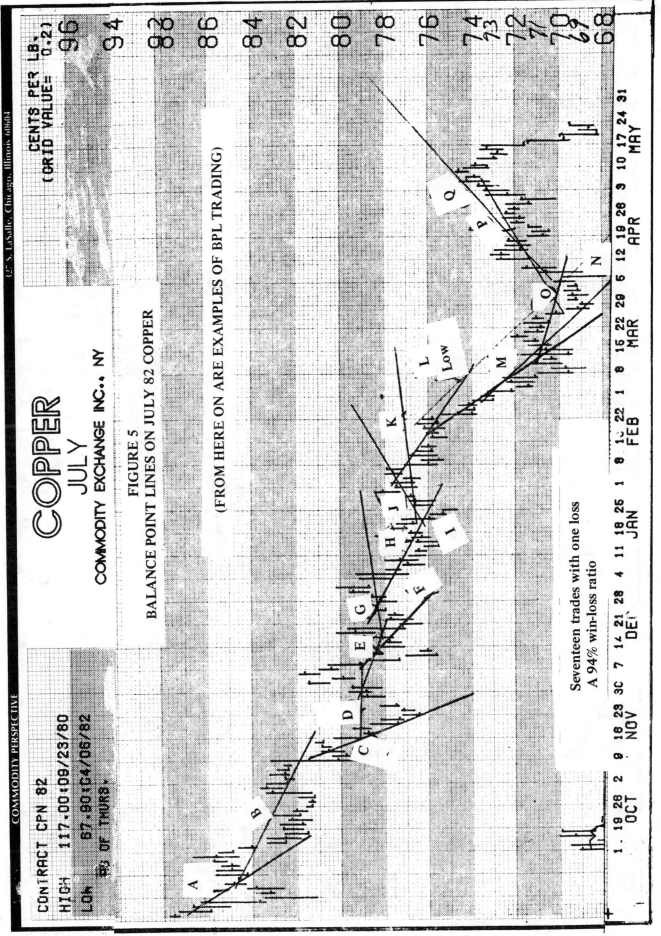

FIGURE 5

BALANCE POINT LINES ON JULY 82 COPPER

(FROM HERE ON ARE EXAMPLES OF BPL TRADING)

Seventeen trades with one loss
A 94% win-loss ratio

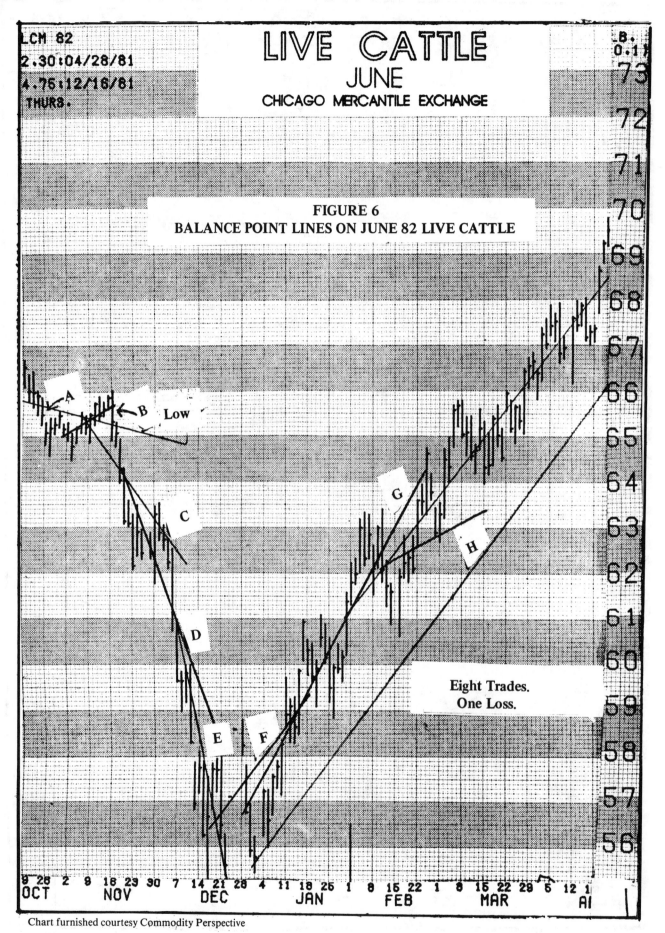

LIVE CATTLE
JUNE
CHICAGO MERCANTILE EXCHANGE

LCM 82
2.30:04/28/81
4.75:12/16/81
THURS.

B.
0.1

FIGURE 6
BALANCE POINT LINES ON JUNE 82 LIVE CATTLE

A

B   Low

C

G

D

H

E   F

Eight Trades.
One Loss.

22

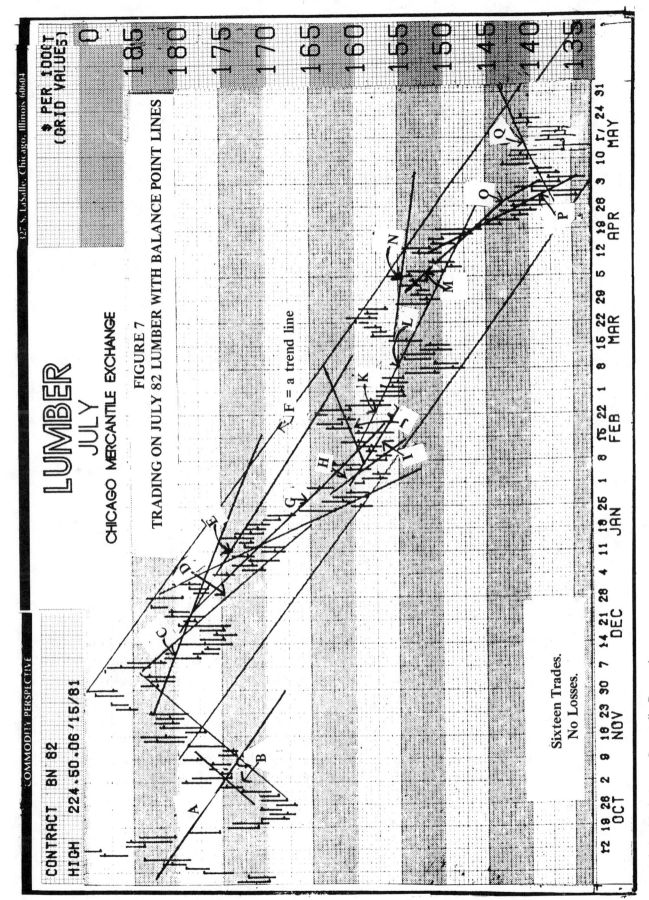

327 S. LaSalle, Chicago, Illinois 60604

$ PER 1000T
(GRID VALUE5)

LUMBER
JULY
CHICAGO MERCANTILE EXCHANGE

FIGURE 7
TRADING ON JULY 82 LUMBER WITH BALANCE POINT LINES

CONTRACT BN 82
HIGH 224.50.06 '15/81

F = a trend line

Sixteen Trades.
No Losses.

OCT   NOV   DEC   JAN   FEB   MAR   APR   MAY

Chart furnished courtesy Commodity Perspective

23

than three losses on one page, which encompassed about six months of price history. Many pages gave a 100% accuracy in testing. Allowing a six cent stop in the grains and about the equivalent of that in other commodities, I was amazed at the times the pivot came very close to the line or to the price extension of the same distance beyond it. I never advocate using only one indicator, but did so here to test only this to see how reliable it was.

BALANCE POINT LINE TRADE BY
TRADE DESCRIPTION RULES TO FOLLOW:

1. Use the last two swings that allow you to extend BPL out where future price will intersect.
2. Trade when price goes through this line.
3. If price stops at the line, and reverses, trade in this direction. Use a six cent stop.
4. Have a running stop loss of profits.
5. Exit when price goes an equal distance on other side of the line. For example, see graph of December Corn, Figure 3.
6. Do not trade congestion.

BALANCE POINT LINE TRADING

1. Look at the December corn example shown in Figure 3. Find the number one balance point line on the left side of the graph. It went through the center of the last two swings. You were expecting price to come down about six cents lower and this was a failure as it did not do so. With price reversing and going more than six cents then closing on its high, you should buy.
2. BPL #2 gave a good sell signal. There may have been a five cent loss against you at one time; and there was a week's wait before price resumed its downward course. You could have found the top of the next swing for this first sell signal by drawing a minor BPL (see dotted line) parallel with line number two which found the top. Had

you been stopped out, this would have given you a second sell signal and would have made money.

3. On BPL #3 you would have gotten in early. Price came back, then slid down the line for two days before giving some nice profits.
4. BPL #4 also would have gotten you in early but eventually paid off.
5. BPL #5 put you in late when much profits were gone, but after the previous large down move there needed to be more confirmation, anyway.
6. For BPL #6 you could have made a smaller BPL shown with the dotted line. The reason is that the swing between lines five and six had a five day reaction going back six and one-half cents. There was no question of this being a pivot, and the last half of the larger swing was a legitimate swing in itself.

With a swing like this where there is more than one small reaction, you need to use channel lines. A BPL down the middle would have had you getting in and out too much without coming back the six cents to the stop loss. See the dotted line in the middle of the channel where the number five BPL goes.

Back to BPL number six, assume you waited for the lower number six line rather than the upper dotted line. You still would have made money.

7. BPL #7 used the middle of a congestion to go down to find the bottom of the next swing. It bumped the line three times before making a good rally. If using a six cent trailing stop loss, you would have been out about 280.
8. BPL #8 gave a good sell signal and BPL #9 was down through the middle of a channel that did not go back more than six cents against you.

BPL TRADING ON GNMA CHART

Start on the left side of the page (see Figure 4) and begin dividing the swings in half. A new swing must have at least a two day reversal to make a pivot for a new swing and possible reversal. With a two day reversal there is reason to make another line, which could put you on the other side of it for another exit method. Stick to our simple rules here, however, of exiting when a line is crossed or when price goes an equal distance beyond the line

25

it crosses.

The first trade is a loss of about six points or $186.00, not counting commission. This is on Nov. 23rd, when price went through the line one day then came back to the next without moving the distance below the line that it had traveled above the line. A day trader would have taken profits early when it went back toward him, but we must count this a loss since it did not reach our objective.

Trade #2 came when the BPL #1 was crossed to the up side, especially since this line had also gone nearly through the middle of the reaction swing of Nov. 23rd. You cover on Nov. 30th for a nice profit.

The BPL #1 also went nearly through the middle of the third swing, so sell when this is crossed again. Take profits on the close, since this is an equal distance below the line. An aggressive trader would have sold again, but we wait for price to come through BPL #2 and buy, taking a loss because it did not make the objective. It gapped through line #2 on the down side, losing about $775.00.

There could have been a very small BPL on the two swings from Dec. 1st to Dec. 4th, but they are so close they are not needed and really qualify for a congestion, which should not be traded (see the dotted line, Figure 4). You go in just under here anyway, at the first chance below line #2 where you made good profits.

BPL #3 really paid off both ways because you gained your objective right at the top of the swing.

With two down days and a close below the congestion you sell again and get out when price fails to make it through BPL #3, which picked the bottom for you. After price reversed on Dec. 24th, staying up for two days, you draw BPL #4. There is no line-crossing to trade until Jan. 4th. An aggressive trader may have taken a trade when price failed to make it to the #4 BPL on Dec. 24th.

Take the trade when price crosses BPL #5 and makes the objective. Now a line could be drawn from the last center, on Dec. 30th, through the other center, of the Jan. 4th swing. There was no trade signal until a congestion was confirmed. Take the high point and the low point of the congestion to get its middle and draw BPL #6. You would trade when price breaks out of the congestion. Then draw BPL #7.

Sell when price goes below the congestion and BPL #7, for a small profit. Here again there could have been a very small BPL over a three day period,

26

but it was still in the congestion. This line would have made a good place for a stop, however. See the dotted line and question mark.

Since there were two days up from the last swing bottom, draw BPL #8 and buy when it is crossed to make a small gain. See the dashed line above the price action from Feb. 5th and 11th. It is not necessary for the BPL's to go through consecutive swings. Just go through two swings so it will intercept price.

You buy when the dashed line is crossed and cover on Feb. 19th when price went an equal distance above this line.

BPL #9 is drawn but it was of little value since price did not come back to it.

BPL #10 put you into a loss when a small congestion was formed.

Number 11 gave an opportunity to sell on Mar. 8th, where you made money; but missed a nice run on down since there was not any line to give another signal.

After some time you can make BPL #12, where you buy when it is crossed, making some good profits.

BPL #13 is now drawn. (See the arrow coming down from above). You sell on Mar. 26th, making another good win.

All that BPL #14 did at first, for the most part, was go across the top of a congestion to keep you out of a trade for the crossing of BPL #15. You buy (on close only) when BPL #14 is crossed with a close above the congestion and have another winner.

Line #16 came out of the congestion and proved to give support for over two weeks, but did not offer a trade.

There was a loss on BPL #17 when you sold on Apr. 14th. It failed to make the gain, then came back through the line on Apr. 15th.

Buy again on Apr. 16th, when it is definite that the line is crossed. But you just about make commission for a breakeven trade. With the third day of the same price range for highs as well as a close to the same price range on the lows, you have confirmation of a congestion.

Finally, a sell signal comes where the old BPL #16 is crossed and you make another small gain.

Draw BPL #18 and buy when it is confirmed that price has closed above it to make another small gain.

There could have been a small line drawn here but a congestion was formed before a trade presented itself.

Balance Point Line Extensions

BPL #19 proved to be the gravity center of the congestion. Then there were three spikes at the top of the congestion. (These are discussed in each of my earlier books). There would have been a good trade on the crossing of the line but are out of date and will not count in the trading results.

Chapter Two

True Trend Lines

INTRODUCTION

Trend lines, an important part of technical analysis, help one to know and remember the trend. The trend may appear to be different to various people, according to how large a time-frame one wants to trade. First, the trader must decide how he is to trade; short term, long term or somewhere in between. It is necessary to constantly keep in mind the size of the market desired; then to know the trend for this size. Those who use intra-day data for five minute charts may only require the trend for the past three days. Of the many techniques in analysis, the one used most often is the trend line.

The drawback of the trend line is that it may change directions before the trader realizes. Trend lines may stay on the same angle, but slide down or move up. There are times when a larger reaction will occur that breaks the trend line, after which it continues on in the same general direction. Some good analysts have made the comment that a trend line usually changes directions three times before the move is actually over. Those who trade trend lines often find that the changing of angles is causing losses. Most long term traders can improve their average earnings considerably if they learn to find the true trend line. I have studied this problem and can report some very promising results.

THEORY BEHIND
THE TRUE TREND LINE TECHNIQUE

From now on, I will call this the TTL, for True Trend Line. This is somewhat like the Equilibrium techniques described in my first book, *Advanced Commodity Trading Techniques.* For those who may not have read this, to make the Equilibrium lines use the pivot as the center and draw an arc of a circle, using the length of the swing as the radius of the circle. Then divide this into halves and thirds (see Figure 8). These Equilibrium lines were good, but they work on a short term basis. For trend lines, a longer period of time should be considered. Since 1979, when this Equilibrium work was done, I have been testing many ideas to find the answers of long term support or resistance recognition.

No genius is claimed in this work; nor are there any visions on the wall telling us what to do. It merely has been a matter of testing over and over and changing, then testing some more. As Edison stated, it is 99 percent perspiration and 1 percent inspiration.

THE SECRET OF A TRUE TREND LINE

The congestion areas, following a break from the previous bottoms or tops, hold the answer to how the market will proceed from there. Generally, it is the first congestion below the previous low, or above the previous high, that is the most important. The other congestions following the first one often help in the analysis, however.

This does not work as good in markets making short swings going in a sidewise manner, such as is seen by triangles, flags or other congestions. Also, the labored move is less reliable, especially if it has evolved from a congestion market rather than from a runaway market or large swinging movement.

HOW TO FIND THE TRUE TREND LINES

When price breaks away from the previous low or high (or from a congestion area), goes a good distance more than previously, then forms a

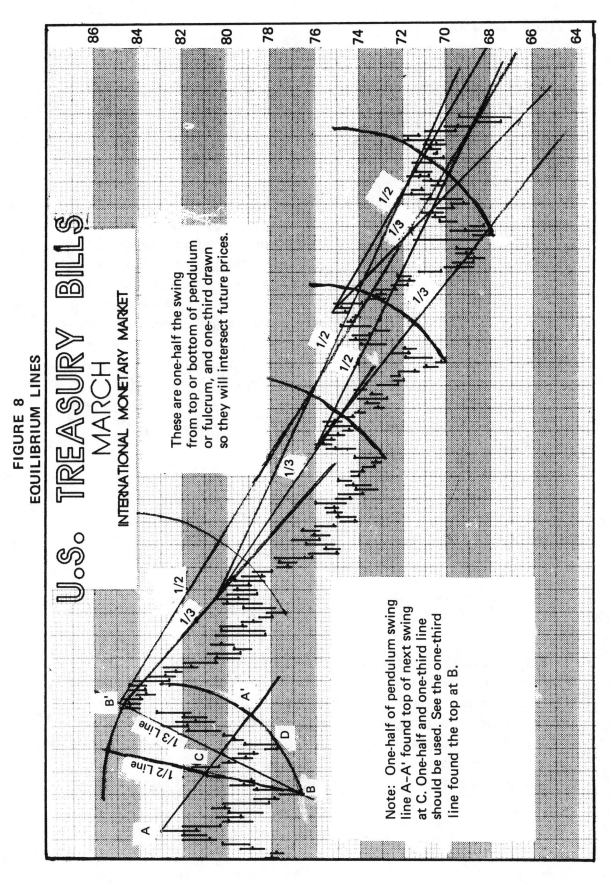

FIGURE 8
EQUILIBRIUM LINES

U.S. TREASURY BILLS
MARCH
INTERNATIONAL MONETARY MARKET

These are one-half the swing from top or bottom of pendulum or fulcrum, and one-third drawn so they will intersect future prices.

Note: One-half of pendulum swing line A–A' found top of next swing at C. One-half and one-third line should be used. See the one-third line found the top at B.

31

congestion, measure the thrust of this congestion. To be a usable trend, the high or low of the previous swing must have been exceeded, or there must have been a clear break from a congestion or choppy area. You can find the high and low of this congestion with dividers to learn the distance of its thrust. Keep the measurement of the thrust of this congestion so it may be used, because this distance is very important. Next, visualize the high, low and sides of the congestion area. Go to the lower corner of the congestion and measure off horizontally the thrust distance that was previously obtained. If this length were preserved on a compass, then it would be easy to make a mark out on a horizontal line from the bottom corner of the congestion area. Do not leave the compass on the high or low, but move it over to the point where the congestion area has terminated and where it can be seen that price is going beyond this congestion. Make sure it is even with the bottom and aligned with the outer edge of the congestion area.

For the first congestion down from the previous low, use the bottom. The bottom rather than the top of this congestion usually works best in a down market; but if a protracted run is developing, the top also becomes important and has predictive value. In up trends, use the top of congestions. Use both on any third congestion down (or up) from the beginning. Here is an example:

"a" is the congestion thrust and "b" is the same distance out from the congestion going from its outer corner. If you see a "TTt," we are going from the top; if a "TTb," we are using the bottom.

To get the main trend line, you must go back to the main high or low. Many charts that are bought do not have room to show the high or low as it may not fit on a page.

Most of the time the TTb will be the true trend. Many times the TTt as well as the TTb will be either support or resistance, turning back price on this line. The TTt is usually not the best of the two on downward moves, but it should be close to the point of return for any wayward movement from the trend.

RESULTS OF TESTING

Out of 200 charts examined, the TTL was on targest 80% of the time. Only large swinging markets are traded. Considering the variety of commodities used, these are very good results. There were times when price came to the TTL, then returned to its previous levels. Up markets found support on the TTL AND DOWN MARKETS FOUND RESISTANCE ON THE TTL.

HOW TO USE THE TTL

This works as a better trend line, but it is also a locator of barrier zones in the market and a directional indicator as well. When trading, always use a number of indicators. It is my firm belief, however, that this will become one of the most important indicators a trader can use. Knowing the True Trend and barrier areas of the market is most vital.

RULES FOR TRADING EXAMPLES

1. Trade when price goes beyond the previous low, high or congestion.
2. Trade only with the major trend (if doing long term trading).
3. Use a stop from $1500.00 to $2000.00. Long term traders must be willing to have larger stops and be willing to see large reactions go against them before they get out.
4. Keep making new TT lines as new congestions are finished. If you are trading long term, use the first TTL for exiting—unless there is a close beyond two pivots with at least three days reaction in each.
5. Intermediate term traders use the new TT lines to exit, then re-enter when there is a close beyond the last pivot. If the long term TT line is

crossed or if two previous strong pivots are passed, then this is considered a change of trend. You then start over again. Do not enter if you seem to be in a congestion or short choppy area.

6. Do not trade any thin markets.

TRADING WITH TT LINES

1. May 82 Corn (see Figure 9).

The first trade using TT lines comes on the break below the previous low on August 5th. This long term trading method would have kept you in the position until September 30th. In at 363 and out at 318, you would have made 45 cents.

TT number 2 found the top of a pivot and was crossed, but did not break above the previous high to give a buy signal.

Note that TT number 3 found the top of a rally.

On November 6th, price broke below its previous low, giving a sell signal. You would have stayed in this trade until January 21st, going from 314 to 281, a 33 cent profit.

2. May 82 Sugar (see Figure 10).

May Sugar broke its previous low on August 4th. If you entered here, there would have been a five day wait, and 25 points was against you at one point, as there was a congestion right on the break. It is necessary to use the first congestion below the break, since you would not have any valid signal for trading until then. This TT line number 1 would have required a disciplined long term trader because it would have kept you in until November 3rd, when there was a close above the line. In at 16.35, out at 12.75. This would have made 360 points, at $11.25 a point.

3. March 82 Lumber (see Figure 11).

This one would have made money, but just not as much. You would have entered a short sale at 187 on August 14th. TTt would have taken you out at 174. TTb would have taken you out at 161 on Nov 17th, making 26 cents.

4. May 82 Copper (see Figure 12).

This would have been a beautiful trade, but most traders would have

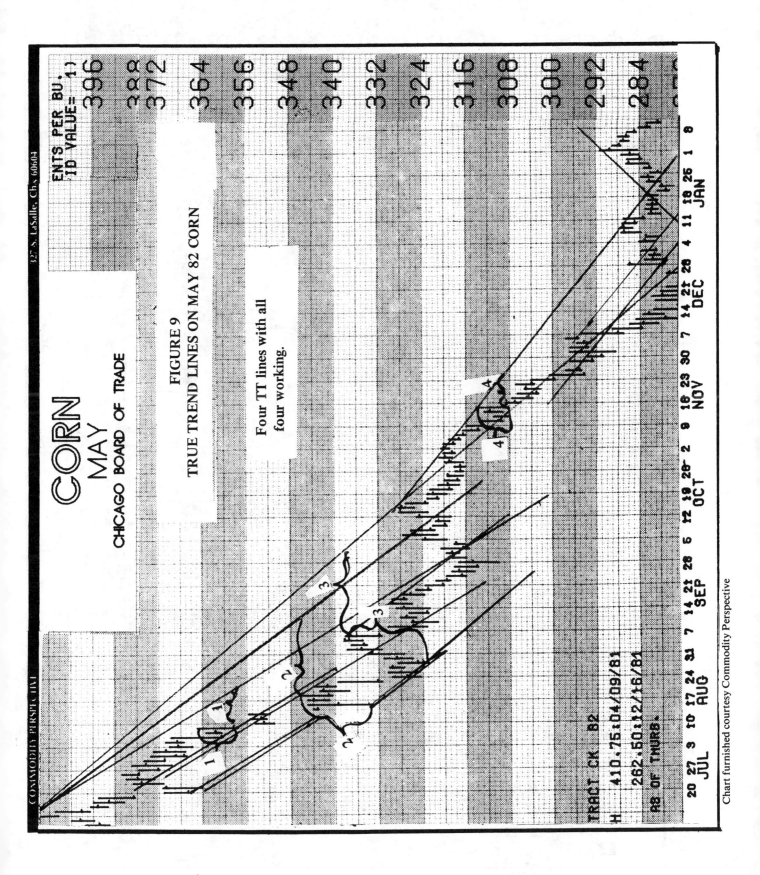

FIGURE 9

TRUE TREND LINES ON MAY 82 CORN

Four TT lines with all four working.

CORN
MAY
CHICAGO BOARD OF TRADE

35

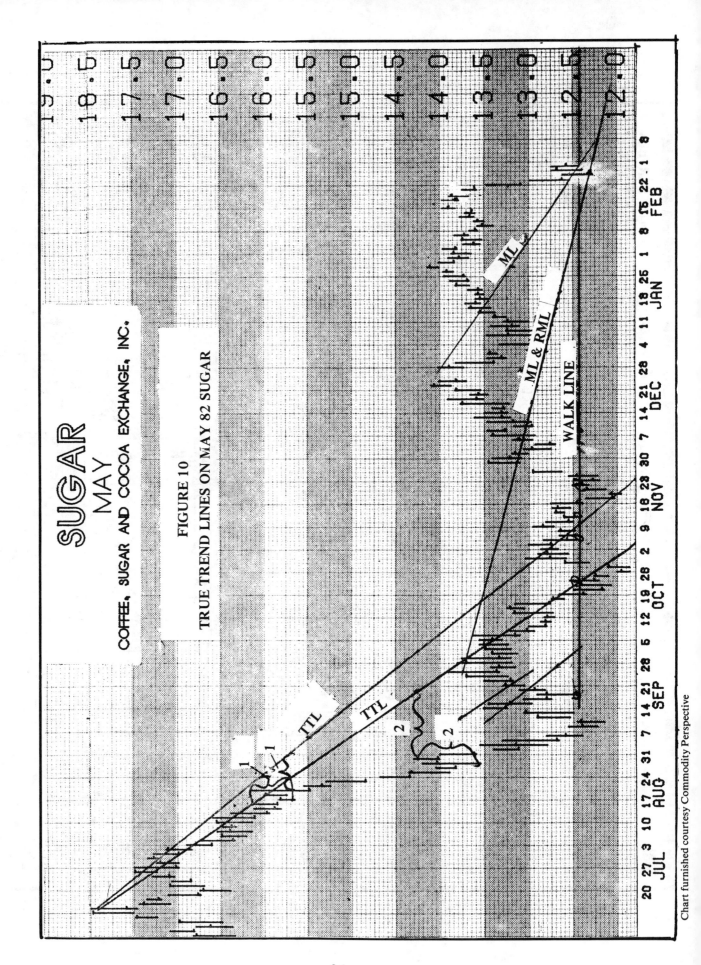

SUGAR
MAY
COFFEE, SUGAR AND COCOA EXCHANGE, INC.

FIGURE 10
TRUE TREND LINES ON MAY 82 SUGAR

Chart furnished courtesy Commodity Perspective

36

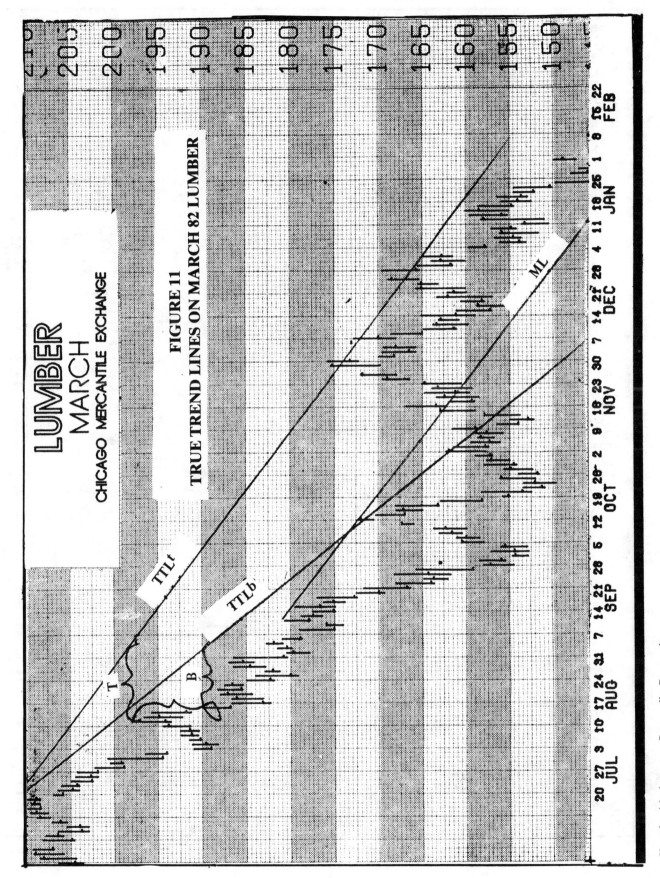

LUMBER
MARCH
CHICAGO MERCANTILE EXCHANGE

FIGURE 11
TRUE TREND LINES ON MARCH 82 LUMBER

37

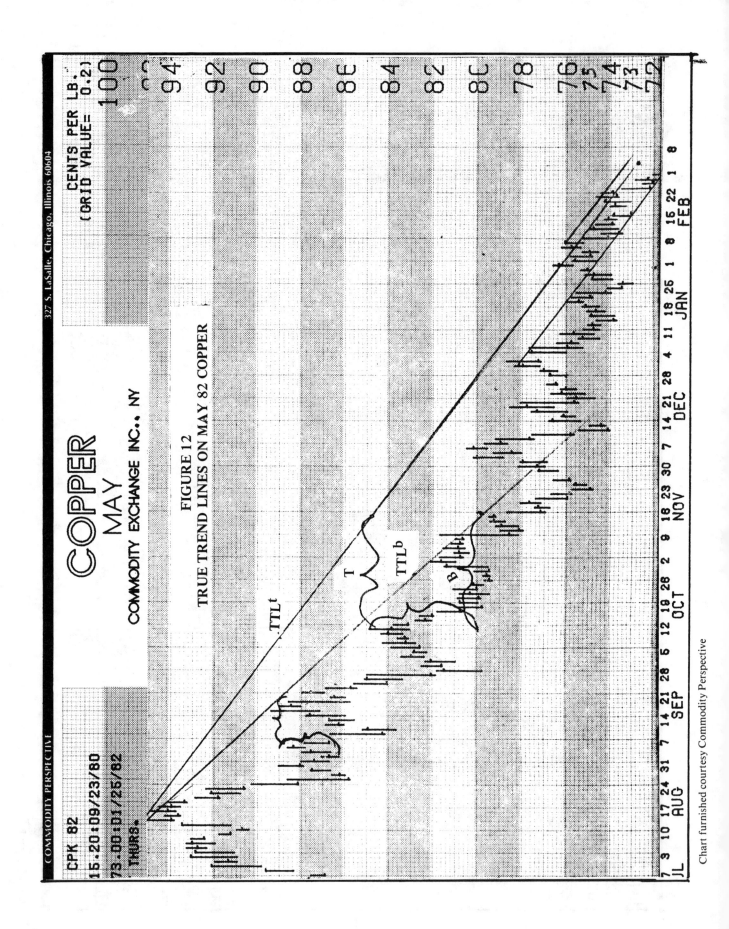

COMMODITY PERSPECTIVE

327 S. LaSalle, Chicago, Illinois 60604

COPPER
MAY
COMMODITY EXCHANGE INC., NY

FIGURE 12
TRUE TREND LINES ON MAY 82 COPPER

CPK 82
15.20:09/23/80
73.00:01/25/82
THURS.

CENTS PER LB.
(GRID VALUE= 0.2)

TTL^t

T

TTL^b

B

38

wanted out on the five cent rallies, I suspect.

You enter when price breaks below the previous low on August 24th, not knowing where the TT line will be since there has been no congestion. With the steep decline, a congestion is imminent and the TT line can be drawn. This kept you in the market until November 30th, when there was a close above the line. In at 88.20 and out at 77.20, you would have made 11 cents at $250.00 a cent. The TTt was used on this. You must decide if you can stand the extra heat to use a higher stop loss. This would have paid off because the TTt was better than the TTb, which would have given a loss. Long term traders should be conditioned to a much longer string of losses or drawdowns than those who trade shorter term.

5.   March 82 GNMA (see Figure 13).

This started with a bad loss. Entering on a break below the low, OCO (on close only), on July 31st at 60.26 and out on close above the short TT line at 61.26 for a loss. You are out, but it's a very frustrating situation as the TT line reversed as soon as it stopped you out for a loss. It is permissible to enter on a close below the next low, which came on August 20th at 59.04. Using the first TT line, you would have been out at 58.28 on the close. Waiting for the second TT line would have caused another loss of four points.

The upward TT line made your money back and more. Going up you are to use the TT top. Under normal conditions, you should use the TTb for down markets and the TTt for up markets. The first congestion was not made until after a close above the previous high. With the market going up so steep so many days in a row, it was not advisable to buy here. The pullback was rather severe, but a congestion occurred between October 14th and 20th. In this case, which is unusual, there had already been a high above the last one, so you can take a trade on the close above the TTt line at 59.20 on October 30th. You are out at 62.28 on December 2nd. You would have made about $3500.00.

There was a close below the first congestion used to draw the first TT line. You could have sold at 61.06. The second congestion made a good second TT line coming down to find the end of the congestion. Using the first TT line, you would be out at 60.13 on the close above the line. The line of the second pivot from the top out to the point of drawing the first TT line is not valid but looks interesting.

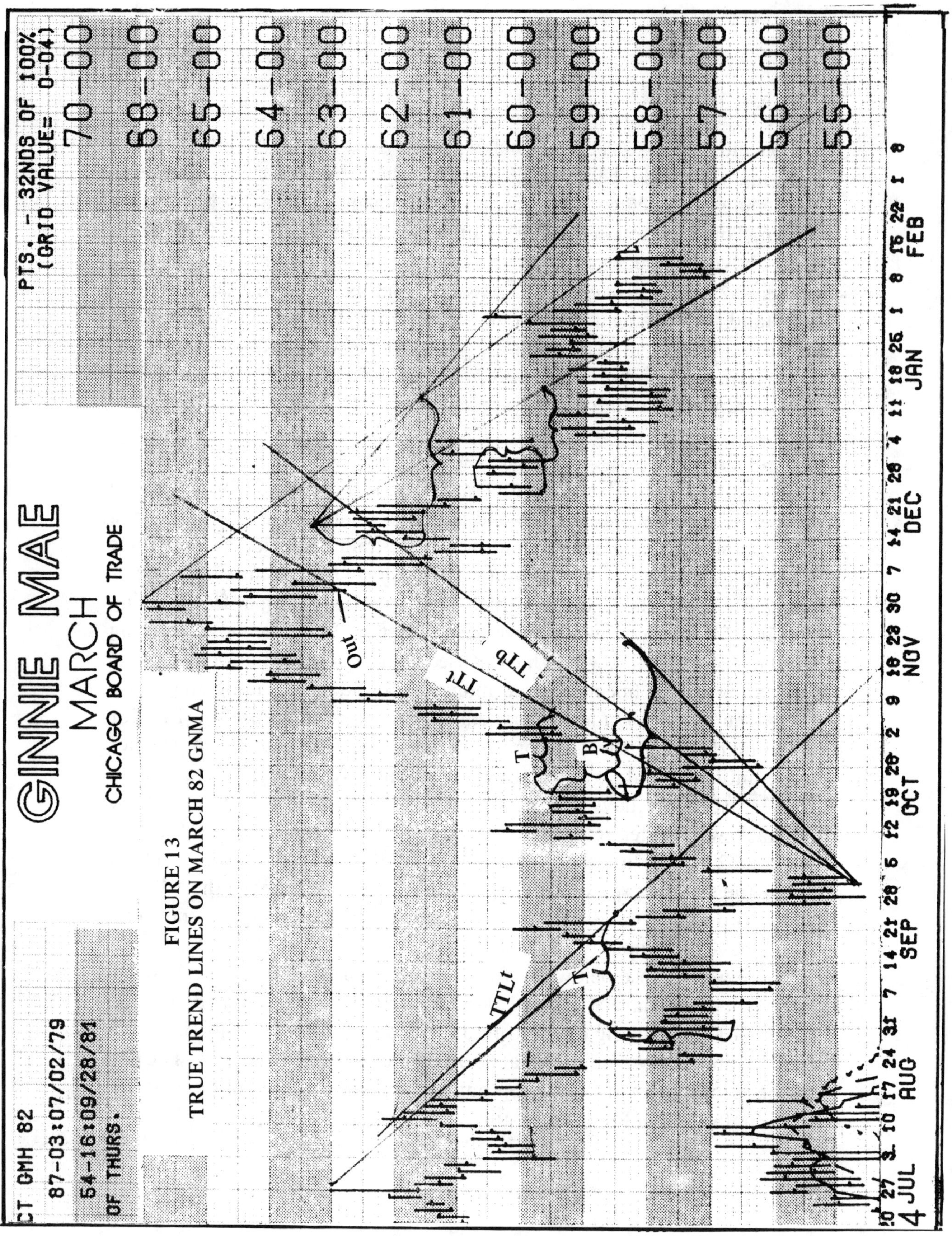

FIGURE 13

TRUE TREND LINES ON MARCH 82 GNMA

Chart furnished courtesy Commodity Perspective

40

6. May 82 Cocoa (see Figure 14).

This commodity is normally thin. It should not be traded the first month or so, giving the Open Interest time to build. Start here on September 24th. You take an immediate loss when price closed above the TT line the next day. After the congestion, price closed on its low just below the congestion on October 6th, where you try another short position. This would have kept you in for a good trade, and no close above any of the TT lines until December 15th. When the market starts churning sideways, you need to use other indicators, as this is a trending tool.

7. March 82 Deutschemark (see Figure 15).

This was an Elliott Flat, or triangle, which should not have been used for TT line trading, although it did give the true trend. After the break from the triangle, wait for a congestion to draw the TT line. You would lose money on this trade, however, as price closed above both the TTb and TTt. Then there was a win entered on the close below the last two closes January 11th, which would have put you even for this commodity.

8. U.S. T-Bills June 82 (see Figure 16).

You can trade the TT lines going down, then with a new high on October 9th you wait for a TT line and trade on the way up. Going down you run into a labored move where channel type trading does better.

9. April 82 Chicago Silver (see Figure 17).

This gives some nice trades, making a lot of money for someone trading long term.

10. April 82 Live Hogs (see Figure 18).

This shows again how often the TT lines hit resistance areas. You could have gone short on the break below the last swing pivot on August 24th and made money. There would have been some heat around September 14th. On the third congestion down, use the TTb.

SUMMARY OF WINS AND LOSSES

I believe this is enough to convince anyone of the value of using TT lines.

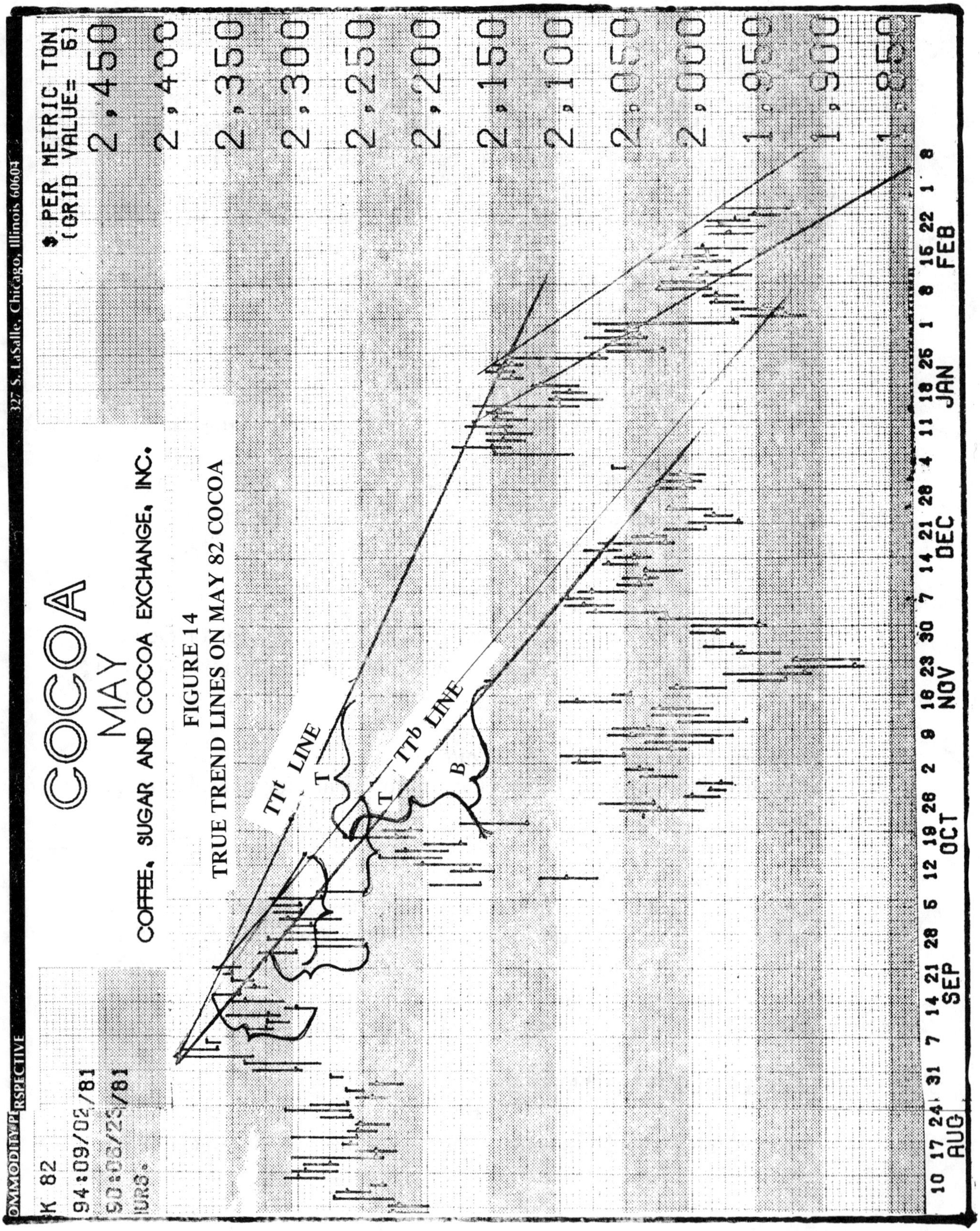

FIGURE 14
TRUE TREND LINES ON MAY 82 COCOA

Chart furnished courtesy Commodity Perspective

42

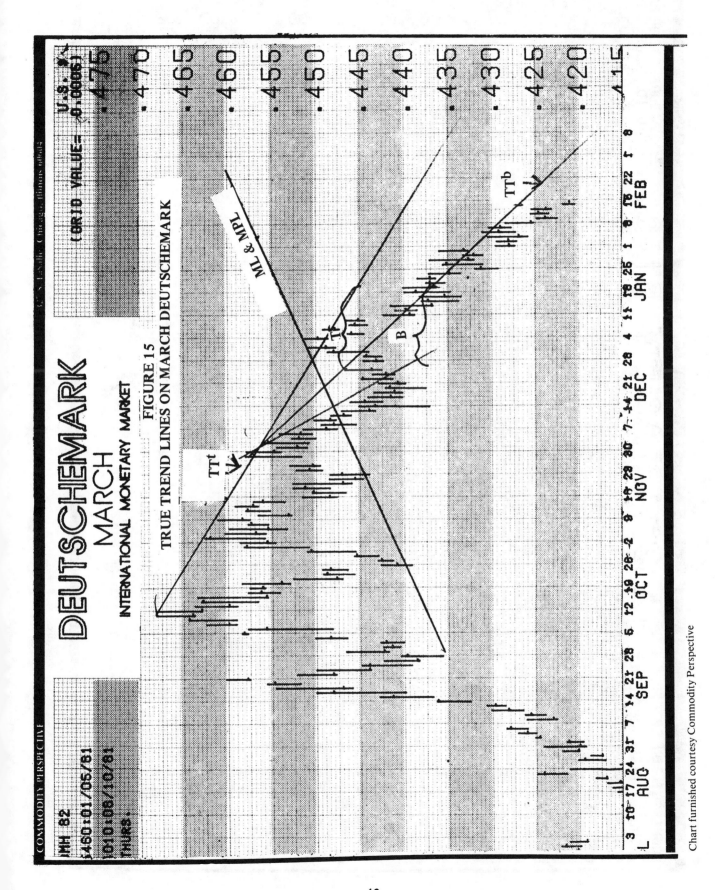

FIGURE 15
TRUE TREND LINES ON MARCH DEUTSCHEMARK

Chart furnished courtesy Commodity Perspective

43

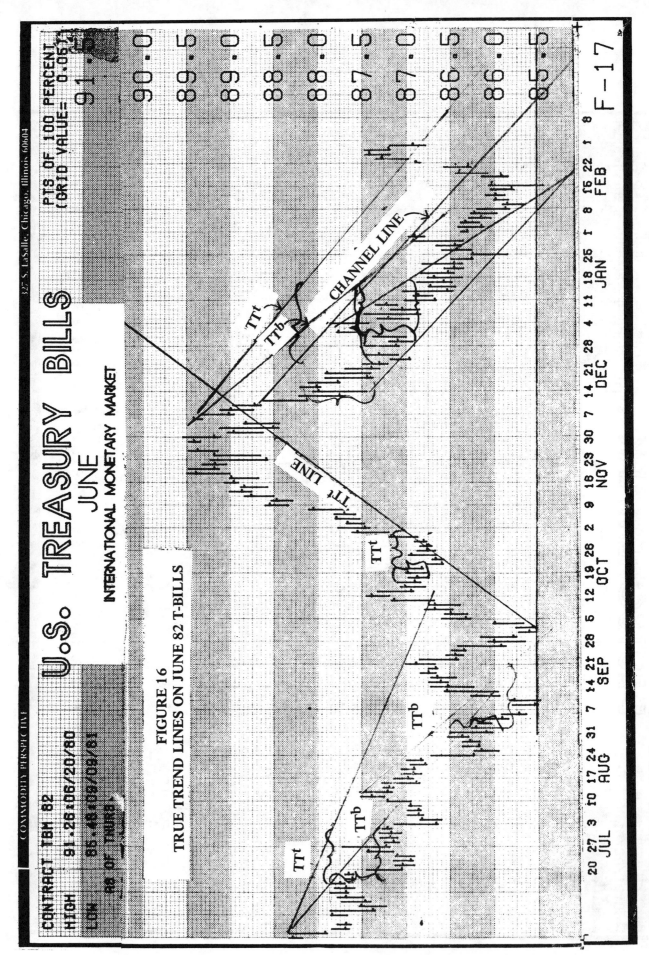

FIGURE 16
TRUE TREND LINES ON JUNE 82 T-BILLS

Chart furnished courtesy Commodity Perspective

44

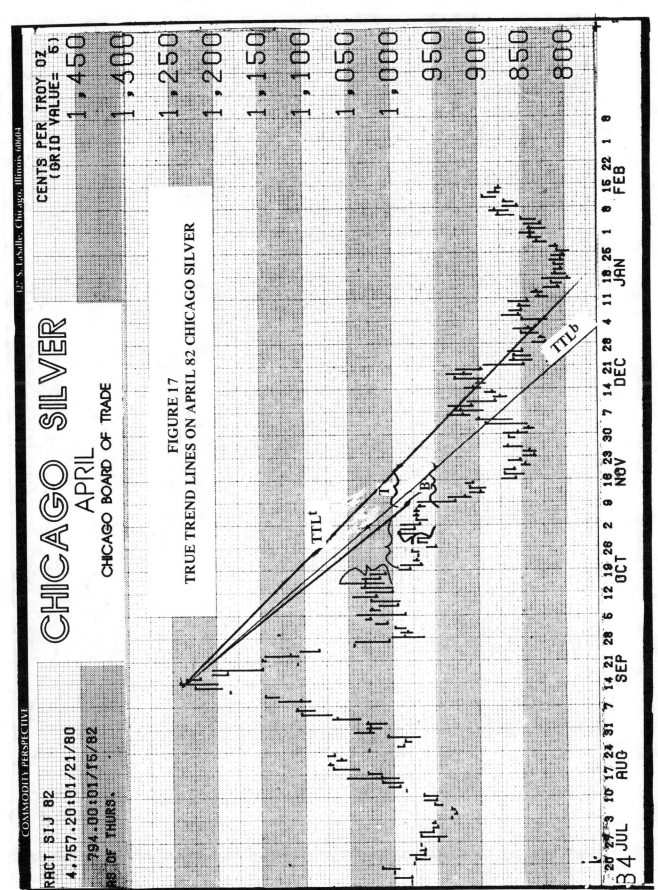

FIGURE 17

TRUE TREND LINES ON APRIL 82 CHICAGO SILVER

Chart furnished courtesy Commodity Perspective

45

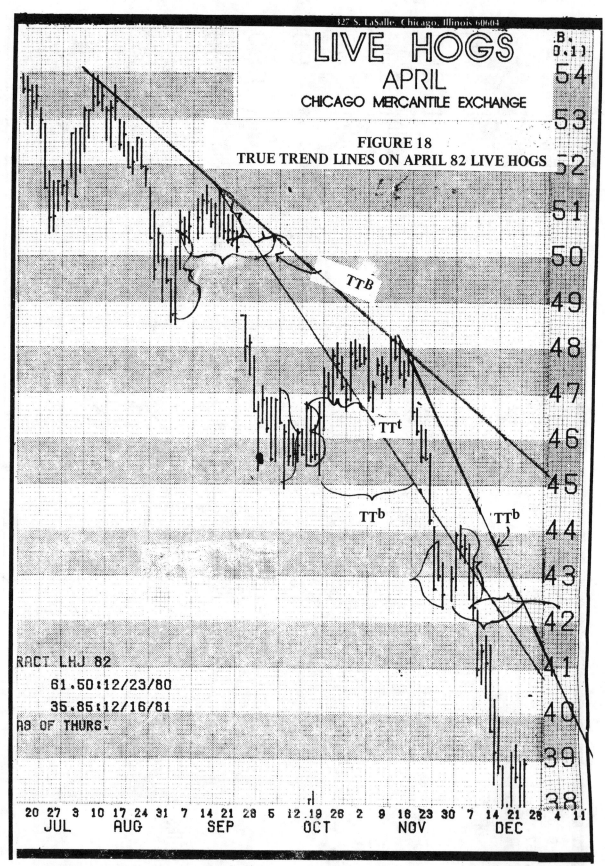

LIVE HOGS
APRIL
CHICAGO MERCANTILE EXCHANGE

FIGURE 18
TRUE TREND LINES ON APRIL 82 LIVE HOGS

TTB

TT^t

TT^b   TT^b

RACT LHJ 82
    61.50:12/23/80
    35.85:12/16/81
AS OF THURS.

54
53
52
51
50
49
48
47
46
45
44
43
42
41
40
39
38

20 27 3 10 17 24 31 7 14 21 28 5 12 19 26 2 9 16 23 30 7 14 21 28 4 11
JUL   AUG   SEP   OCT   NOV   DEC

Chart furnished courtesy Commodity Perspective

46

I do not recommend the use of one indicator, but, if I had to use only one, the True Trend Line would be it for long term trading. Since the trades were merely to teach what is being done, I am making no effort to give a summary; but it is plain that good money would have been made.

Chapter Three

Gravity Lines

INTRODUCTION

Looking at a chart one often notices price continuously fluctuating around a certain area. Have you often thought that it would be nice to have known this in advance? This problem has intrigued traders for years. Now I may have found a way to do this; at least my tests have been very favorable.

THE THEORY INVOLVED

1. The laws of action-reaction are based upon the principle of finding a gravity center. Equal price action is expected on the opposite side of the center as was found before the center. Andrew's Median Lines are based on this theory. The Median Line is expected to give the end of a swing, or to be one-half of a swing if the line is penetrated.[*]

There are a lot of other indicators based on the principle that every action of the market will produce an equal reaction in its opposite price action. Gann used a forty-five degree line marked on charts that were scaled to a one-to-one ratio. The forty-five degree line divides the chart action in half and is accurate in many cases.

---

[*] This is explained in the book *"Eight New Commodity Technical Trading Methods"* by J. D. Hamon, 1982.

One can do even better, however, by considering the length of the swings and the size of congestions as well as the distances between congestions.

2. Relative strength is incorporated into the use of gravity lines. Look at Figure 20, which shows examples of gravity lines. Note that the angle of the line is controlled by the distance between pivots. The angle is also controlled by the space between a pivot and a congestion as well as by the size of the congestion.

Any time there is a fast market, without much churning, this is reflected in the lines; or if the market goes from one congestion to another rather rapidly, this will also affect the lines.

The lines help indicate the strength of the market. They are much better than the ordinary speed lines often used by traders who pick some arbitrary percent of the range to use for drawing their lines. Gravity lines let the market tell you where the lines should be and relate them directly to what the market is doing.

WHY THIS THEORY IS RELEVANT

1. Analyze the Pivot Finder Lines described in my past work (see Figure 19). Note that the lines are an equal distance apart, and hit all the congestions and pivots for a period of six months. Transfer the line in the middle, which hit a congestion, and draw a parallel line at the top, as shown in the figure.

It is the same length, and found a pivot when on a parallel line with the middle one. The theory used in Gravity Lines is similar, except simplified by keeping only the part that is needed for the present price action. Pivot Finder Line theory made the Gravity Lines come as a logical next step in development.

2. Lots of testing has shown that, in general, any price below the lines has a stronger pull to the down side. Once the lines have been decisively broken, the pull is up until new gravity lines can be made which are pointing down. These then exert a downard force on the market. It is one of the best indicators of relative strength. The old theories of action-

FIGURE 19
PIVOT FINDER LINES

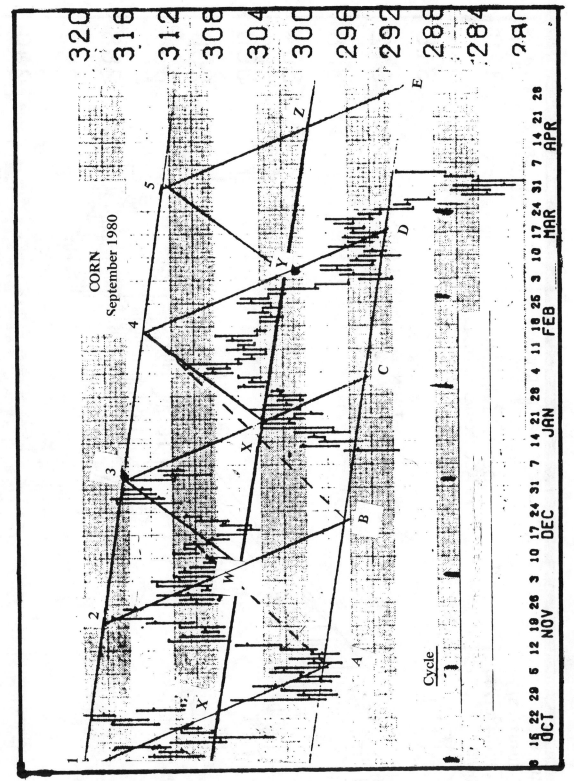

CORN
September 1980

Cycle

Chart furnished courtesy Commodity Perspective

51

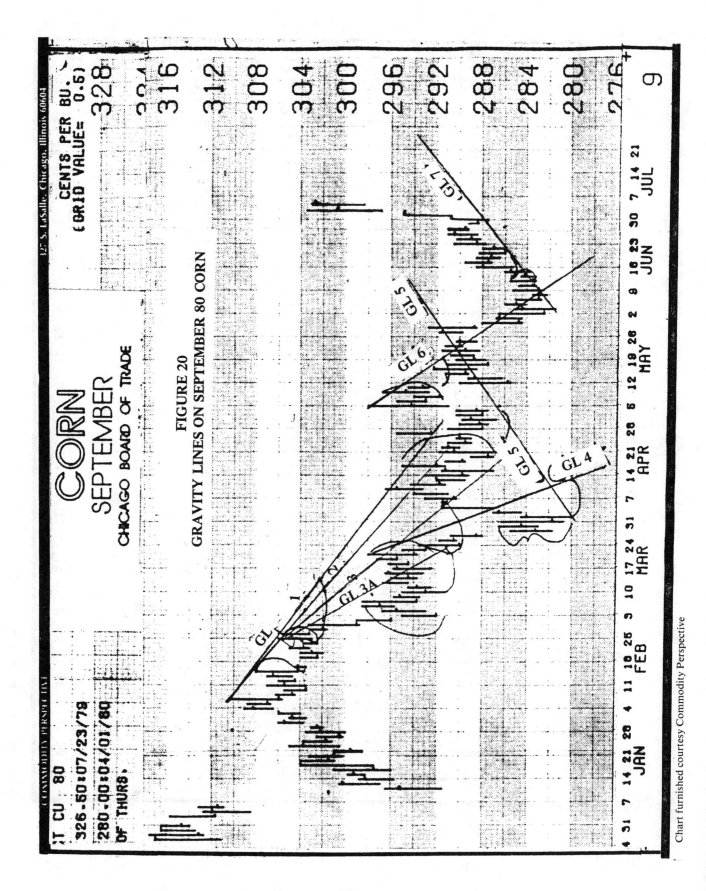

FIGURE 20

GRAVITY LINES ON SEPTEMBER 80 CORN

Chart furnished courtesy Commodity Perspective

52

reaction and relative strength are combined into the action of the market to give information not to be found elsewhere.

WHAT OTHERS HAVE DONE

There have been various formulas used, such as zero balance, key indicator, and Gann clusters to find the gravity center of the market.

After studying Gann, I found that he was right in saying that the market often moves in multiples of a number. The number working most often is seven. If you add seven to—or subtract it from—a high or low, you are often close to a turning point or congestion. This also applies to multiples of seven, such as 21.

Gann's squaring of time and price is another way of finding balance in the market, except in this theory the pull of gravity is between time spent in a move and the length of the price move. It is a different way of using the gravity of the market to predict price changes.

Cycle work and channeling are other ways of trying to find what causes the market to change when it does, and involves the use of gravity pull or thrust in the market.

HOW TO FIND THE GRAVITY CENTER OF A MARKET

1. *General Information*

It must be kept in mind that there are several gravity centers of a market, according to the length of time involved. Daily price fluctuations may have gravity centers not apparent on weekly or monthly market movements. Not only the length of time must be considered, but also the type of market. Channels and congestions quite obviously have their centers as the pull and thrust of the market. Intra-day data may have its own small pulls, but all markets and data time periods must be considered by the type of market involved. A runaway market is much different from a congestion. Also, the swinging markets must be considered separately. A lot more random movement is found in the smaller data time periods. It is best to start with the larger data periods first, but nothing can be finalized without identifying the kind of market.

2. *Kinds of Markets*

a. Congestions, and channels or labored moves, will usually fluctuate around a center line through the middle of the congestion or channel.

b. Swinging markets must be judged by the length of the swings and congestions involved. Use Balance Point Lines on these markets to find gravity centers.

c. Runaway markets are the hardest to predict using ordinary techniques, but it is much easier if Gravity Lines are employed. So the Gravity Lines are primarily for use in trending markets (or running markets).

HOW TO DRAW THE GRAVITY LINES

There must be a swinging or trending market, with some congestions along the move. Measure the vertical distance of the congestion and divide this in half. Take this distance and measure out horizontally, starting where the congestion appears to be ending. Draw a line from the last pivot through this point—measured out from either the top or bottom of the congestion (see Figure 21).

Draw the gravity lines, then find the point of price activity furthermost from this line to draw a parallel. Now divide this distance in half and you have the true gravity center of this market. Should the gravity line parallel be broken, new lines need to be drawn. This will not happen often, only in very fast moving markets.

TRADING GRAVITY LINES

A. *Definitions*

1. **Up-Pivot** This must have at least three days of higher highs, followed by at least two days of lower lows.

2. **Down-Pivot** It must have at least three days of lower lows, followed by at least two days of higher highs.

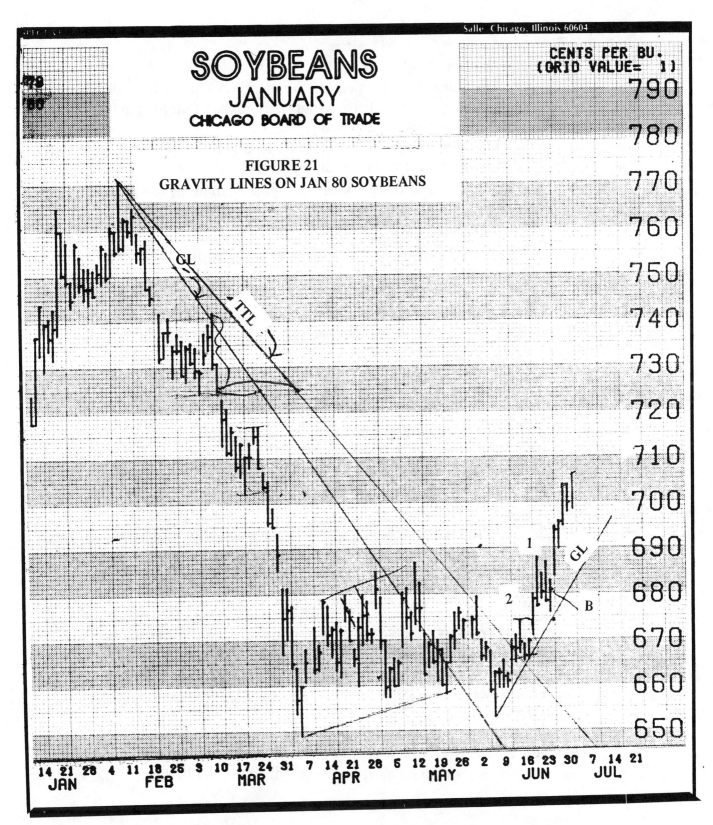

SOYBEANS
JANUARY
CHICAGO BOARD OF TRADE

Salle Chicago, Illinois 60604

CENTS PER BU.
(GRID VALUE= 1)

FIGURE 21
GRAVITY LINES ON JAN 80 SOYBEANS

Chart furnished courtesy Commodity Perspective

55

3. Congestion

a. Any sideways movement of the market taking at least three days is a congestion. There cannot be more than four days up in a row, or four days down in a row.

b. The swings may move down or up on a small angle, but if they are in a churning sideways motion, this is a congestion.

4. Change of Trend
This is when price goes beyond the last pivot—either a low or high.

5. Use of Gravity Lines

a. In a down market, use the bottoms on the first two congestions.

b. On the third congestion in a down market, use the top of the congestion for marking to draw the line.

c. In an up market, use the top of the first two congestions and the bottom on the third.

B. *General Rules*

1. Do not put on a position or add to any position if the market is near the gravity center. In an up market, buy only when price is in the lower half of the gravity line boundaries; and in a down market, sell only when the price comes back to the upper half of the gravity line area.

2. It is necessary to always trade with the trend. It is identified by the passing of a previous pivot.

C. *Entrance/Exit Rules*

1. Enter only when there is a change of trend, confirmed by a break beyond the previous pivot's low, high, or congestion.

2. Exit when price penetrates the Gravity Line. Consider the trade good as long as it stays between the gravity line and its parallel, and better if price is below the gravity center line.

3. Reenter in the same direction when price closes beyond a new congestion. Draw a new gravity line with each new congestion and use this one, with its parallel, as the new boundaries for trading.

PROBLEMS THAT MAY BE ENCOUNTERED

I am using only gravity lines and their parallels because this is necessary to test their validity. But there are times when one does not find a congestion with which to make the gravity lines. On other occasions, the congestion is part of a top and indicates that further sideways action is expected. See the first part of the September Corn chart, Figure 20, for an example of this.

Most of the time the rules given above are best, but there are times when using both the top and bottom of the congestion helps. So far there is no rule to identify this in advance. Our rules work and are helpful, but there are exceptions. Note the January Soybean Chart, Figure 22, as an example.

The rule to use is to go from the top of the congestion on the first part of an up movement, and from the bottom on the first part of a down movement. We always urge everyone to test things for themselves. Everyone should develop his own style. As the years go by, things may change. The basic theory given above is sound, and it has been successful to my complete satisfaction.

WHAT TESTING HAS PROVEN

After investing a great deal of work and time, I've found evidence to prove that the congestions found in a market are related to what follows in price action.

1. Congestions close to pivots or turning points of the market denote further churning until there is a close beyond the limits of this sideways price action.
2. Most of the time these lines will extend out to find pivot points much later in the market, or support or resistance areas.
3. The Gravity Lines make good channel boundary lines.

DIFFERENCES BETWEEN GRAVITY LINES
AND TRUE TREND LINES

The angle of the Gravity Line is one-half of the True Trend Line angle. A lot of line bumping or crossing may occur on the Gravity Lines, but this

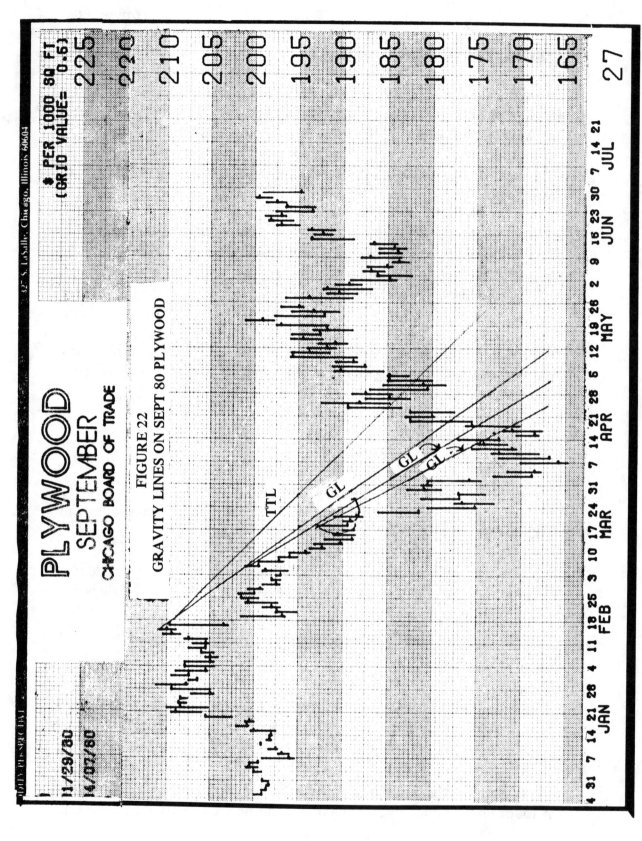

FIGURE 22
GRAVITY LINES ON SEPT 80 PLYWOOD

Chart furnished courtesy Commodity Perspective

58

seldom happens on the True Trend Lines unless there is a change of trend. The True Trend Line is a good trend indicator, but the Gravity Line is not, even though both are governed by the distance between congestions and the range of these congestions. It could be compared with moving averages, where one is one-half the size of the other. The manner of finding the Gravity Lines or True Trend Lines is much better, however. The distance between congestions and the range of congestions is directly related to what price action is doing. It is not some number pulled out at random, as is the case with most moving averages. This makes the Gravity Lines and True Trend Lines much more meaningful for trading indications.

The Gravity Line was given that name because it is usually the line closely followed by price action. The True Trend Line will often find the tips of reactions or rallies, but the Gravity Line is more apt to be part of a channel. When price goes through a Gravity Line, ordinarily it only goes an equal distance on the other side, then a reaction occurs and price resumes its old line of travel for a time. Lines drawn parallel to the Gravity Line on the other side of price action usually form good channel lines that may be traded for some time.

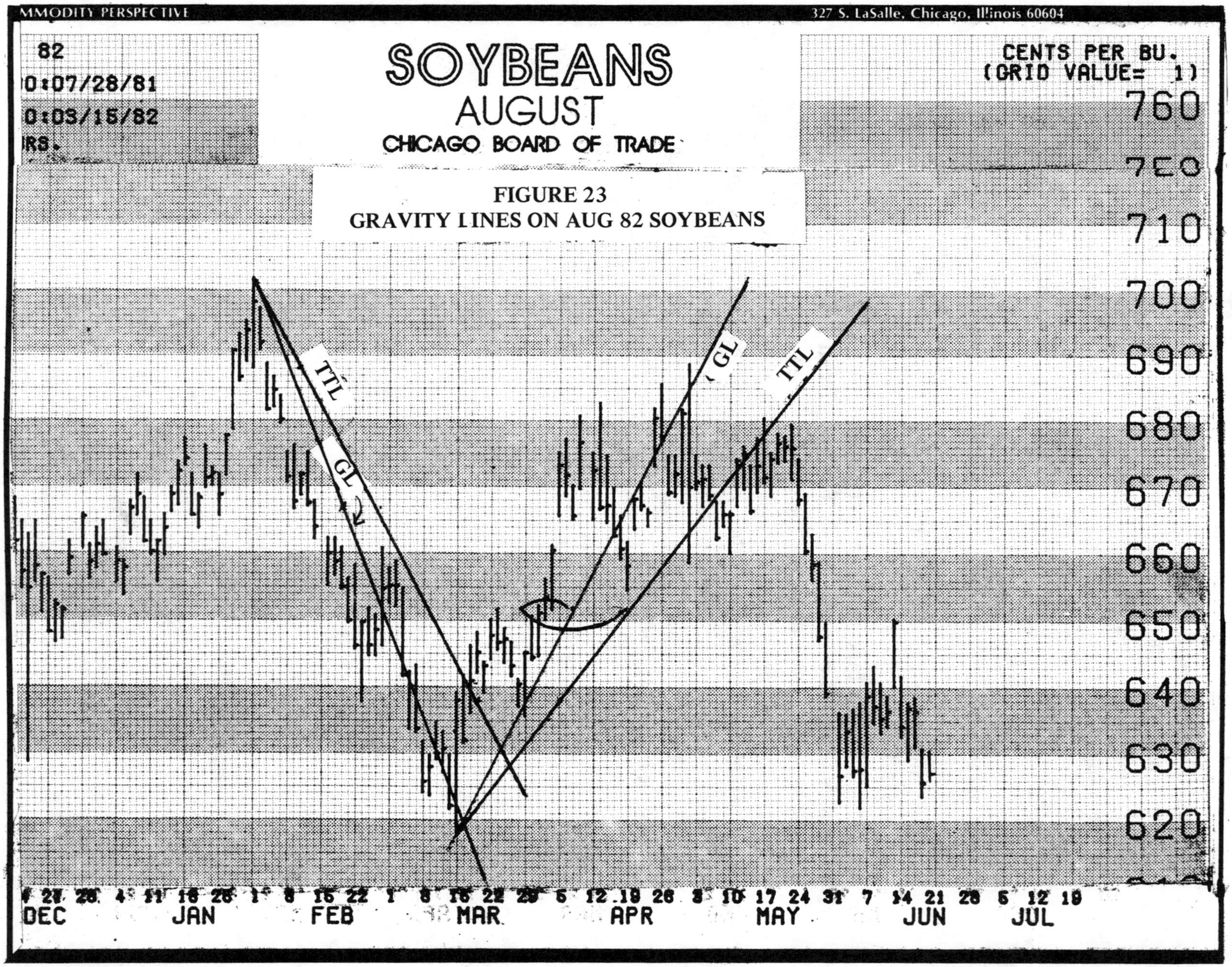

SOYBEANS
AUGUST
CHICAGO BOARD OF TRADE

FIGURE 23
GRAVITY LINES ON AUG 82 SOYBEANS

Chart furnished courtesy Commodity Perspective

60

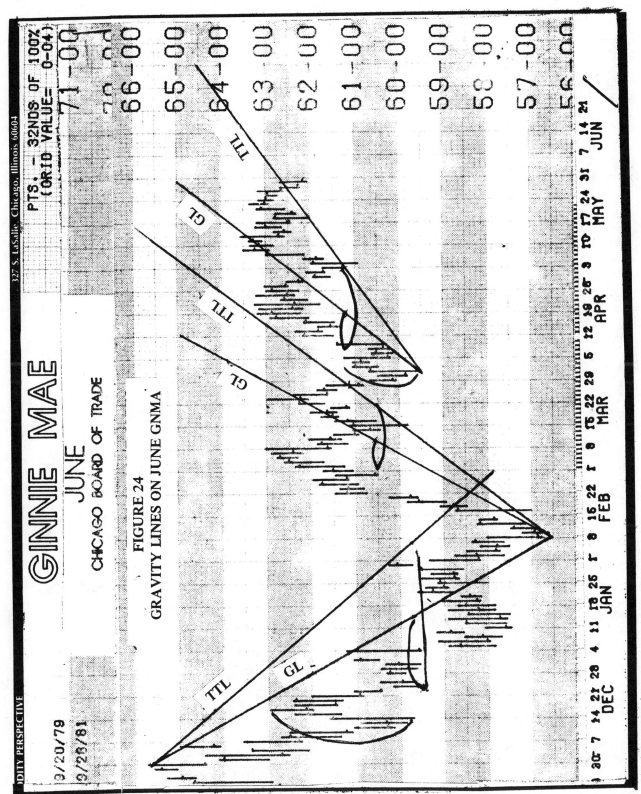

GINNIE MAE

JUNE

CHICAGO BOARD OF TRADE

FIGURE 24
GRAVITY LINES ON JUNE GNMA

61

Chapter Four

TH Lines

MEANING

The "TH" is an abbreviation for thrust. The range of a swing is used to make the TH lines and represents the "thrust" behind the move. This trading technique is designed to find the end of a move and also to forecast pivots that are several months away.

HOW TO MAKE TH LINES

Get the measurement of the range by finding the high and low of a swing with dividers or some other measuring tool. Take this measurement, which is found on the vertical lines of price charts, and then lay it over on the horizontal. Go to the point where this last swing penetrated beyond the previous swing's pivot point. Starting at the point of this penetration of the last swing, put the left side of the dividers down where the price went through, then mark the swing or thrust distance out on the horizontal date line away from the price line. See examples of this in Figure 23.

Always use the point of penetration beyond the last swing pivot. The TH line is brough down from the top pivot through the point marked as the equal distance of the thrust of the last swing; or it may come up from the bottom through the point where the thrust's distance is marked on the "date line." There is no question about the length of the thrust (or range) between the last swing's high and low. This requires only simple measuring and drawing of horizontal lines. The results have proven to be good.

THE THEORY OF TH LINES

These lines are a simplification of the "Square of a Circle" technique taught in *"Advanced Commodity Trading Techniques,"* by J. D. Hamon (see Figure 24). TH lines take the main, and confusing, functions out of this while retaining some of its theory with this easier method. In the "Square of the Circle" procedure, a lot of work was required, but the only help to the trader was the part where price was intersecting the lines. This is a short cut way to get a lot of its value quicker.

WHAT TH LINES WILL DO

These are Barrier Lines, in that price has a hard time penetrating them. I have tested several hundred in all kinds of markets. They have been found to be helpful in finding future pivots and the bottoms or tops of a market. This gives the trader knowledge of where to expect the market to be months ahead of time.

A NEW SPEED LINE

The TH lines are also variations of speed lines, which have been in use for many years. The difference is that the TH lines use the distance of the thrust or range to measure horizontal distances, and do not bisect them into thirds or halves as is done with speed lines (see Figure 25).

HOW TO USE THE TH LINES

These lines are good for finding resistance or support areas where they are intersected by price action. Usually, as price hits one of these lines, this

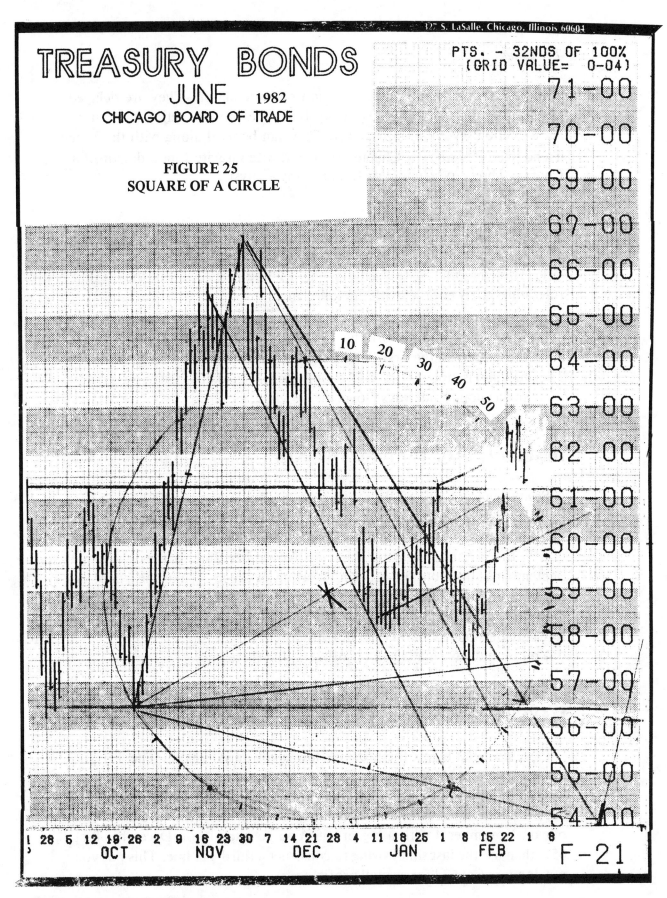

65

will be a turning point in the direction of price action. They are delayed trend lines, and usually move away from the present action to that of future action several months away. They can be used along with the True Trend lines, described in Chapter Two, and with Gravity Lines, described in Chapter Three, to help in long term trading analysis.

RULES FOR TRADING TH LINES

1. These are almost the same as the TT line rules. Use all the TT line rules unless they conflict with the following:

    a. Each time there is a new swing having at least five days in it, you draw a new line and use this for trading. Enter with the main breakthrough when the first TH line can be drawn.

    b. This is not for trading choppy markets like congestions or any short choppy sideways move.

DESCRIPTION OF TRADING TH LINES

See the chart of July 82 Wheat (Figure 26), but ignore the TT lines.

Price closed below the last swing low on November 18th, but did not get below the main swing low until November 23rd. The TH line is drawn here and is the distance from the high on November 2nd to the low made September 28th. Note the brackets labeling distances. Take this space on the dividers and place one point on the chart at 445 on November 23rd, where the main breakout occured. The TH line is drawn from the top down to where the point is market out horizontally.

You should have made good profits trading these lines.

MARCH 82 SOYBEANS (See Figure 27)

Price dropped below the previous low pivot on August 5. The TH line drawn from this small swing hit almost exactly on the longer swing marked TH1. You can draw a second smaller TH line using the range from 686 to 720, which occurred from October 12 to October 21. This would get you out on November 4 with a big profit. You go back in on December 8 at 651, then use the last small swing to construct a third TH line. This put you out January 6 at 634 for a small profit.

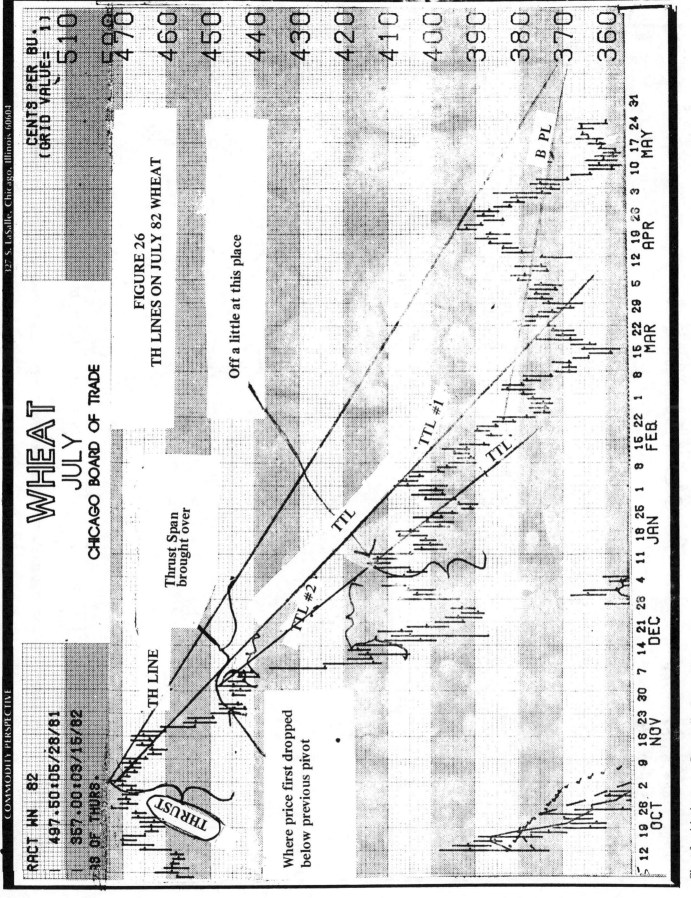

FIGURE 26
TH LINES ON JULY 82 WHEAT

Off a little at this place

Thrust Span
brought over

Where price first dropped
below previous pivot

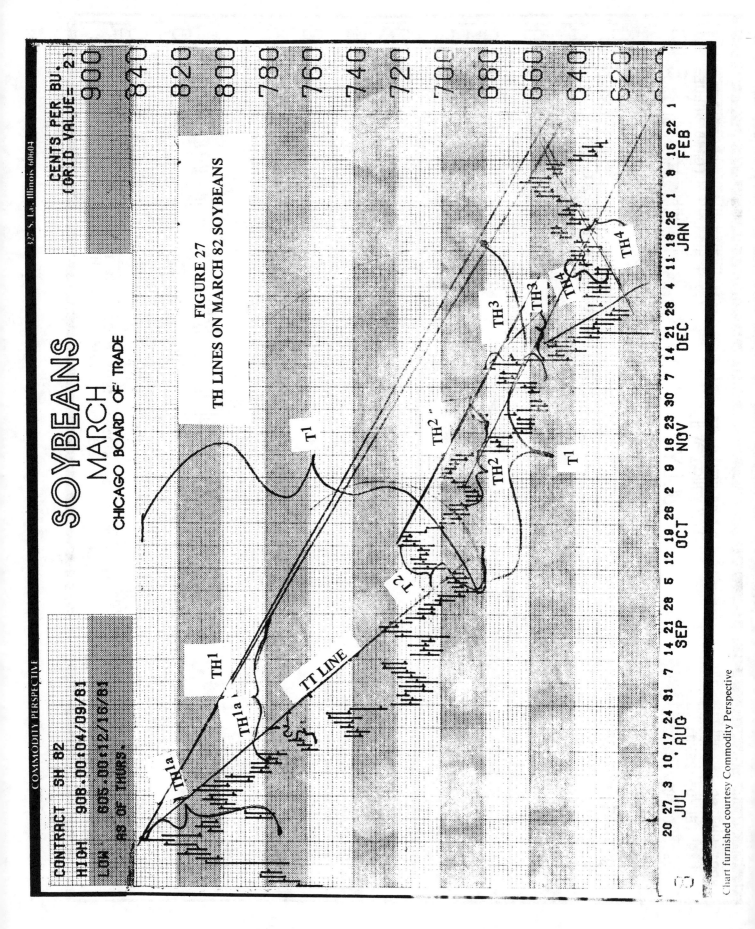

FIGURE 27

TH LINES ON MARCH 82 SOYBEANS

When price goes above the previous pivot on January 5, you have a change of trend. TH 4 makes a perfect trend line. You take profits of about ten cents on this up swing.

MAY SOYBEAN MEAL (See Figure 28)

The first part of this chart was so thin most traders would not trade here. The dashed TH line shows a TH line drawn from the first swing. If someone had been brave enough to trade this thin market, he could have gone short on the break below the previous pivot on August 10 and stayed in until February 1 when the dashed TH line was temporarily broken. TH line #2 would have left him in to go on down for more profits.

Those preferring shorter term trading can trade the TH lines of smaller swings and make good money.

This is not meant to be an exact in-and-out trading history. It is just to illustrate the value of the TH lines. Use them! They will give you a lot of help in your trading.

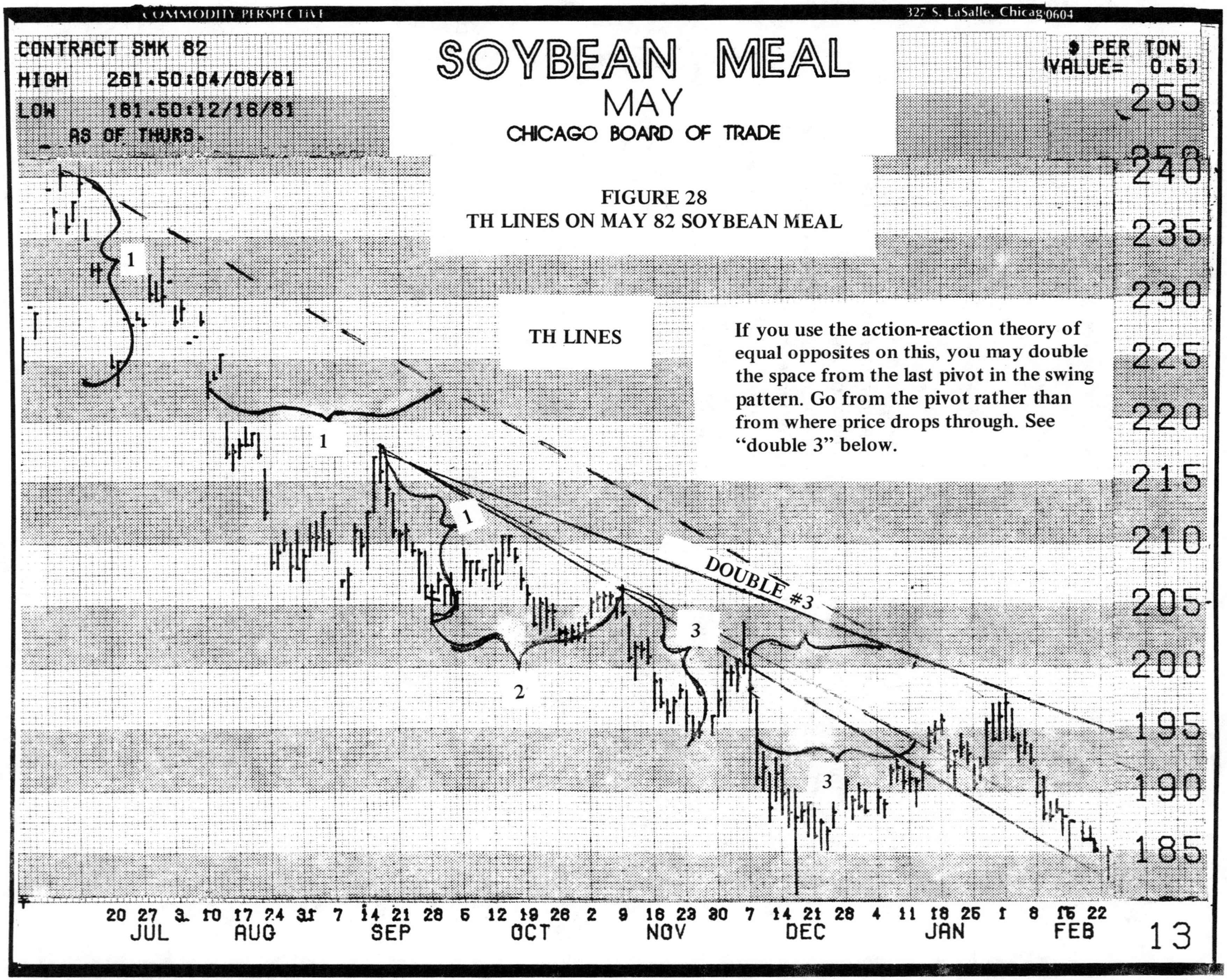

FIGURE 28
TH LINES ON MAY 82 SOYBEAN MEAL

SOYBEAN MEAL
MAY
CHICAGO BOARD OF TRADE

CONTRACT SMK 82
HIGH 261.50±04/08/81
LOW 181.50±12/18/81
— AS OF THURS.

TH LINES

If you use the action-reaction theory of equal opposites on this, you may double the space from the last pivot in the swing pattern. Go from the pivot rather than from where price drops through. See "double 3" below.

DOUBLE #3

70

Chapter Five

Hamon's Congestion Method

I. HOW TO MAKE MONEY IN CONGESTIONS

1. Different markets require a different kind of strategy. Use a special strategy for congestions.
2. Have precise and rigid definitions of terms and rules.
3. Make allowance for more random movements, since this is short term trading.
4. This plan keeps one in control at all times, but it must be followed exactly.
5. Be consistent in everything.

II. WHEN TO TRADE

1. Wait for all rules to be validated.
2. It is necessary to wait until the price requirements are met.
3. On congestions that are in runaway and swinging markets, trade only with the trend until a change of trend is confirmed by two higher highs (or lower lows).

III. GENERAL INFORMATION

1. This method can work even when using $10,000 or less. Since congestions that meet the following requirements do not come up very often, use a switch plan for this when a valid congestion is found. In other words, use something else as your primary trading system, with this as a backup when a congestion occurs.

2. Keep charts to help you look for the pattern required to denote the beginning of a congestion.

3. This has been tested on three years of data using all the main commodities. Simulated trades are shown for educational purposes and may be slightly more or less when actually trading.

4. If conditions are met, this method buys on the bottom of the congestion, then covers under its exit rules. Stop and reverse is used after the third swing, but never after the fifth swing when price may break out.

5. The exit rules should be enough of a stop for most people, but anyone may put in a stop below the previous low or above the previous high if desired.

IV. SPECIFIC TRADING RULES

1. Definitions

  a. Congestions

(1) The price pattern must have more than two up and down days in each swing. See Figure 29 where it is marked that it is too tight starting on April 5.

(2) When trading in a down market, there must be two pivots on the bottom with one in between. These pivots may be short swings of more than two days each, but no more than five. If the market has been going up, there must be two pivots on the top part of the forming congestion and a down swing or pivot in the middle of these two. The congestion must have its highs in the same general price range. After a congestion is established, a long range day may make up for two or more of the previous short range days.

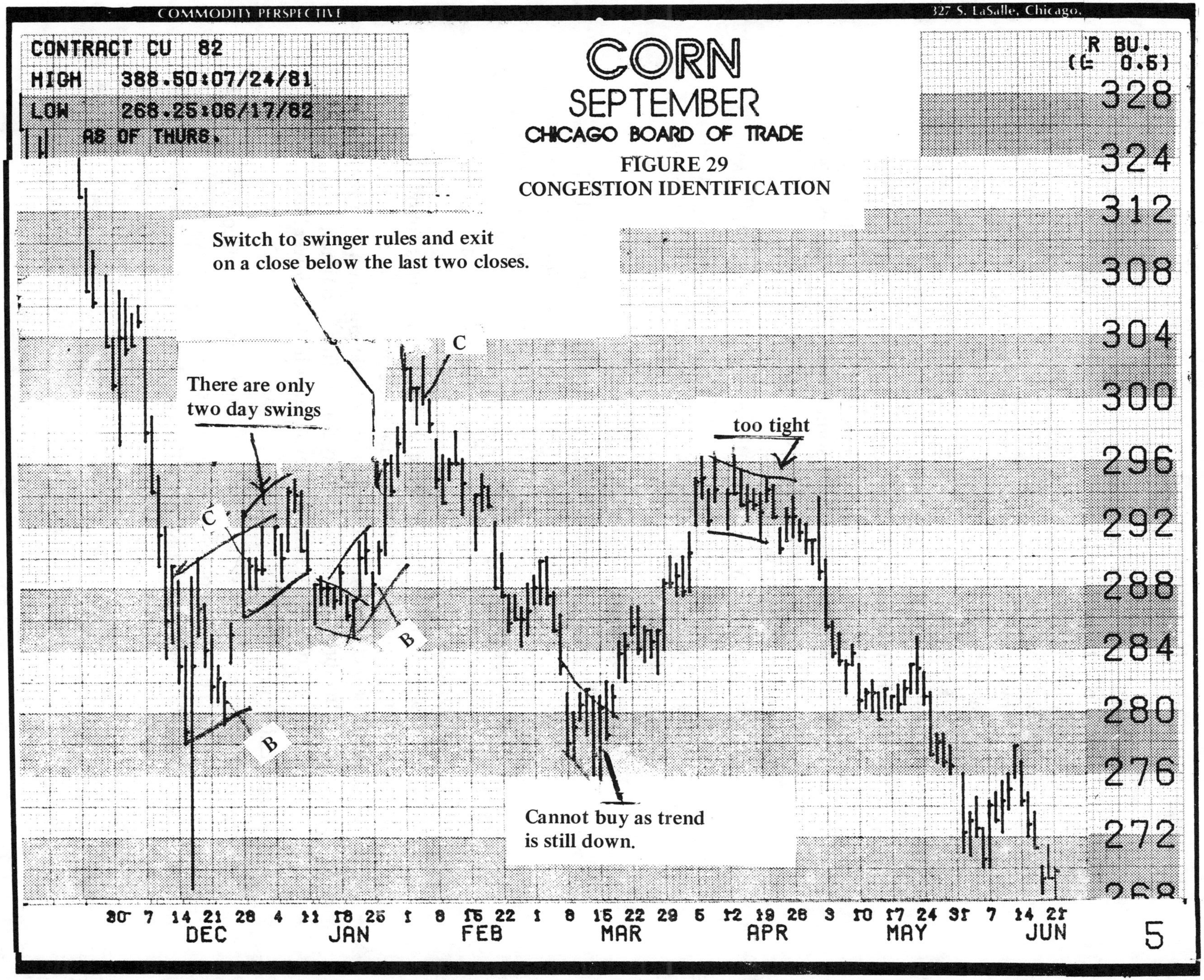

CORN
SEPTEMBER
CHICAGO BOARD OF TRADE

FIGURE 29
CONGESTION IDENTIFICATION

CONTRACT CU 82
HIGH 388.50:07/24/81
LOW 268.25:06/17/82
AS OF THURS.

PER BU.
(¢ 0.5)

Switch to swinger rules and exit on a close below the last two closes.

There are only two day swings

Cannot buy as trend is still down.

too tight

73

(3) After the second lower low (or higher high), draw the line at the top with its parallel at the bottom; or the line at the bottom going by the two pivots, with its parallel at the top off of the center pivot.

(4) Always use the last two pivots for your lines. Keep changing them as necessary.

(5) It is okay for this to be on a small slope. It still qualifies as a congestion.

b. Breakout Rules

(1) If there are more than five days in a swing either up or down and the boundaries of the congestion have been surpassed by 20% of the range of the congestion, this is a breakout. See the price action on January 29 in Figure 29.

(2) If the previous swing before the congestion has more than 62% of its range retraced and the boundaries of the congestion are exceeded by more than 20% of the congestion's range, this is a breakout. See December 28 and April 2 in Figure 29.

2. Rules for Entering the Market

a. All the above rules must be met, plus the range must be large enough for profits. To test if the range is large enough, take 40% of the congestion's range, subtract this from the range length, and see if the amount left is enough.

b. Enter not more than 20% of the range away from the bottom line or top line.

c. You never trade the first two swings; and if this is following a swinging or runaway market, do not trade the first three swings. On these market types you are required to trade only with the trend or the swing direction of the runaway for the first two times, or until a change of trend is confirmed by two higher highs or lower lows.

3. Exit Rules

a. For the first two swings after the congestion has been confirmed, use the penetration of the previous day's close as your exit signal.

b. For the rest of the trades, use the close below the last day's close to exit.

4. Breakout Rules

   a. On swinging markets or breaks going into a swinging market, change the exit to be a close beyond the previous two closes.

   b. On runaway markets or breaks turning into a runaway, use the close beyond the last four closes.

   c. If a definite labored move emerges, use the bottom line to exit if long, or the top line to exit if short.

5. Difference Between the Labored Move and the Congestion

   a. The congestion moves more sideways than the labored move.

   b. The labored move stays in a definite slanted channel, with the channel slanting at least thirty degrees. There must be at least four swings to verify a labored move.

   c. Most congestions will not have more than six swings, whereas the labored move should last for several weeks.

   d. Some congestions will turn into labored moves, and it is possible to see a labored move swing back to make an irregular congestion. Always follow the line of the last two pivots until a pattern is definite, then trade only from the bottoms or tops of the channel.

6. Difference Between Swinging and Runaway Markets

   a. A fast five (or more) day run, then a congestion, denotes a runaway type market.

   b. When the angle of travel is almost straight up (or down) for five days, consider this a runaway and not a swinger.

   c. If a market has been traveling a long way for a period of two or more months, then the market reverses and makes a gap, consider this a breakaway gap and the beginning of a runaway in the opposite direction. A second gap close to the first gives further confirmation that this is a runaway and will go a long way. See Figure 30 on June 19 and 21.

V. HOW TO OPTIMIZE AND CHANGE WHEN YOU HAVE TOO MUCH COMPANY— AVOIDING THE CROWD OF LOSERS

1. The entrance from the lines can be altered from 20% to either 15% or 25%.

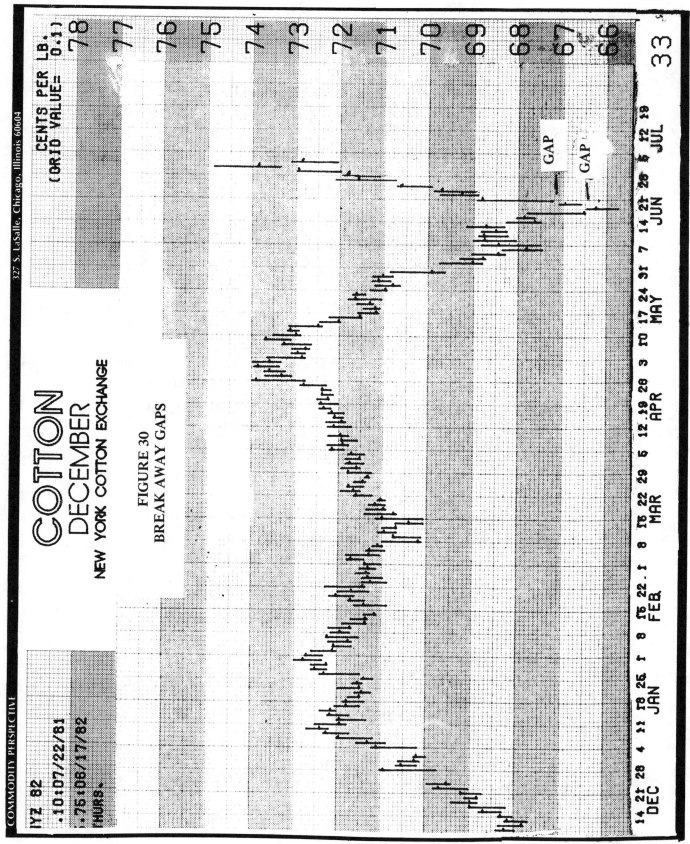

COMMODITY PERSPECTIVE

327 S. LaSalle, Chicago, Illinois 60604

COTTON
DECEMBER
NEW YORK COTTON EXCHANGE

FIGURE 30
BREAK AWAY GAPS

IYZ 82
.10:07/22/81
.75:06/17/82
THURS.

CENTS PER LB.
(GRID VALUE= 0.1)

2. You can change the exit to be beyond various amounts of previous closes; and it can be on-close-only to give further variation. Right now, this will not make as much money, but as trader sophistication rises, variations will be more profitable.

3. After three pivots are made on the bottom (or top), you may enter with the trend at under 50% of the range.

KEEP IN MIND!

In actual trading there will be times when the market will go through the congestion, running your stops rather than turning as it had previously been doing.

When a congestion is first forming it is hard to tell whether or not it will be the kind where one can make money. These rules and examples should help, but keep in mind that actual trading is different from a strategy planned by using historical data.

Paper trade with this at first. You may find you'd like to make a few minor changes. Remember, with this type of trading there is a lot of randomness. So a technical system must have flexibility.

See the congestion marked out in Figure 31. There are ten grids between the lines, which represents $2500.00 for this contract. The rule is to buy 20% above the line and cover when price goes back beyond the previous close. Put a stop beyond the lines when first entering a trade. You would have sold on Mar. 17th at 800 and been out the next day about 780. You buy on Mar. 19th at 770 and go out Mar. 23rd at 795. You sell on Mar. 24th about 803 and get out on Mar. 26th at 783. Buy on Mar. 29th at 770 and go out the next day at 780. You would have made a total of 75 points, at $50.00 a point, for a total estimated profit of $3750.00 not counting the deductions for commissions. In the congestion marked in Figure 32, the range is eleven grids at $50.00 each. 20% of $550.00 is $110.00, so you have a possible $330.00 room for profits. You buy at 166 on Feb. 10th but are kicked out the next day at 167. Sell at 170 on Feb. 12th and get out on the 16th at about 168. Sell on Feb. 23rd at 170 and go out on the 25th at 166.50 for a total estimated profit of $650.00 before commissions.

FIGURE 31
TRADING CONGESTIONS IN DEC 82 CHICAGO SILVER

Chart furnished courtesy Commodity Perspective

78

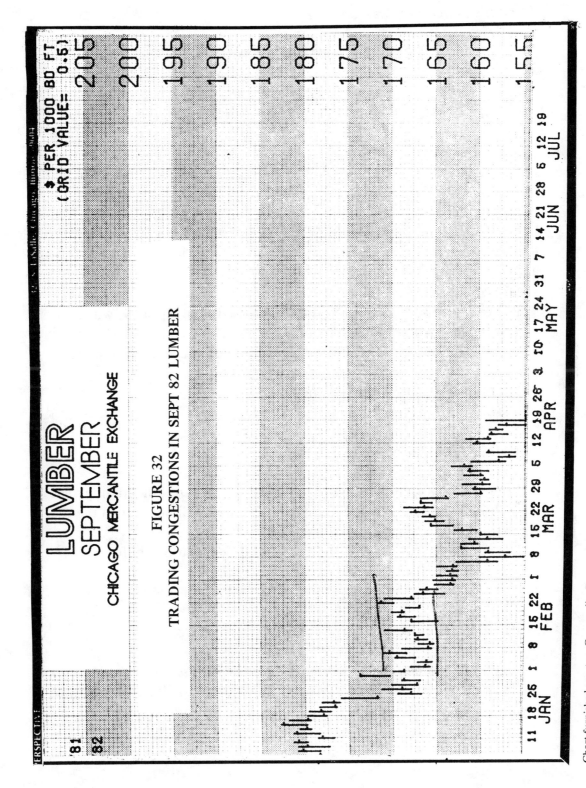

LUMBER
SEPTEMBER
CHICAGO MERCANTILE EXCHANGE

FIGURE 32
TRADING CONGESTIONS IN SEPT 82 LUMBER

79

TRADE-BY-TRADE DESCRIPTION

JULY 82 OATS (See Figure 33)

Buy on November 11 on the close. This is with the trend, since price had previously gone above the last two congestions or pivots. You cover near the 0-2 line at the top. Since the trend is up for the first two trades, you must only buy; so you buy again near the 0-2 line on November 24, covering near the top again. Now you can sell on the way down. The 0-2 line has been working and you buy again on December 2 and cover near the top line. This is four wins in a row.

There is not another congestion that qualified until April 19, when you buy. You put in a stop and reverse on April 20. You could cover when price penetrates the two previous closes, or stay in to sell a second contract, since price did not get very close to the top line.

The total score is nine wins and no losses!

JULY 82 SOYBEANS (See Figure 34)

After the 0-2 line is drawn on January 14, it is just routine trading. The second trade did not go far, but the third one went sailing through the top for extra profits.

The next congestion started out okay, but ended up too tight for trading.

There are five wins and no losses.

SEPTEMBER 82 CANADIAN DOLLAR (See Figure 35)

There wasn't much congestion here. There are two sell trades going with the trend. The last one zipped through the bottom 0-2 line for some nice profits.

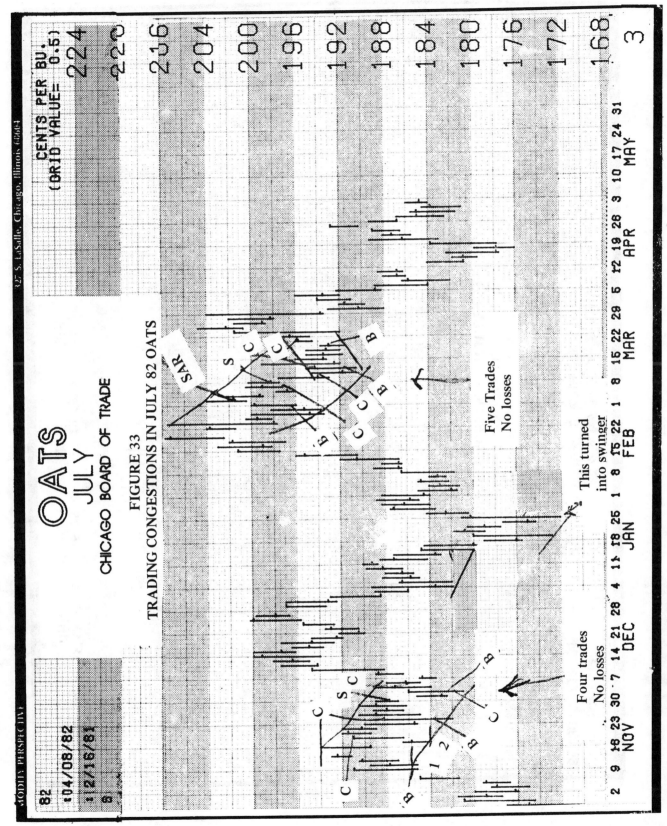

FIGURE 33

TRADING CONGESTIONS IN JULY 82 OATS

81

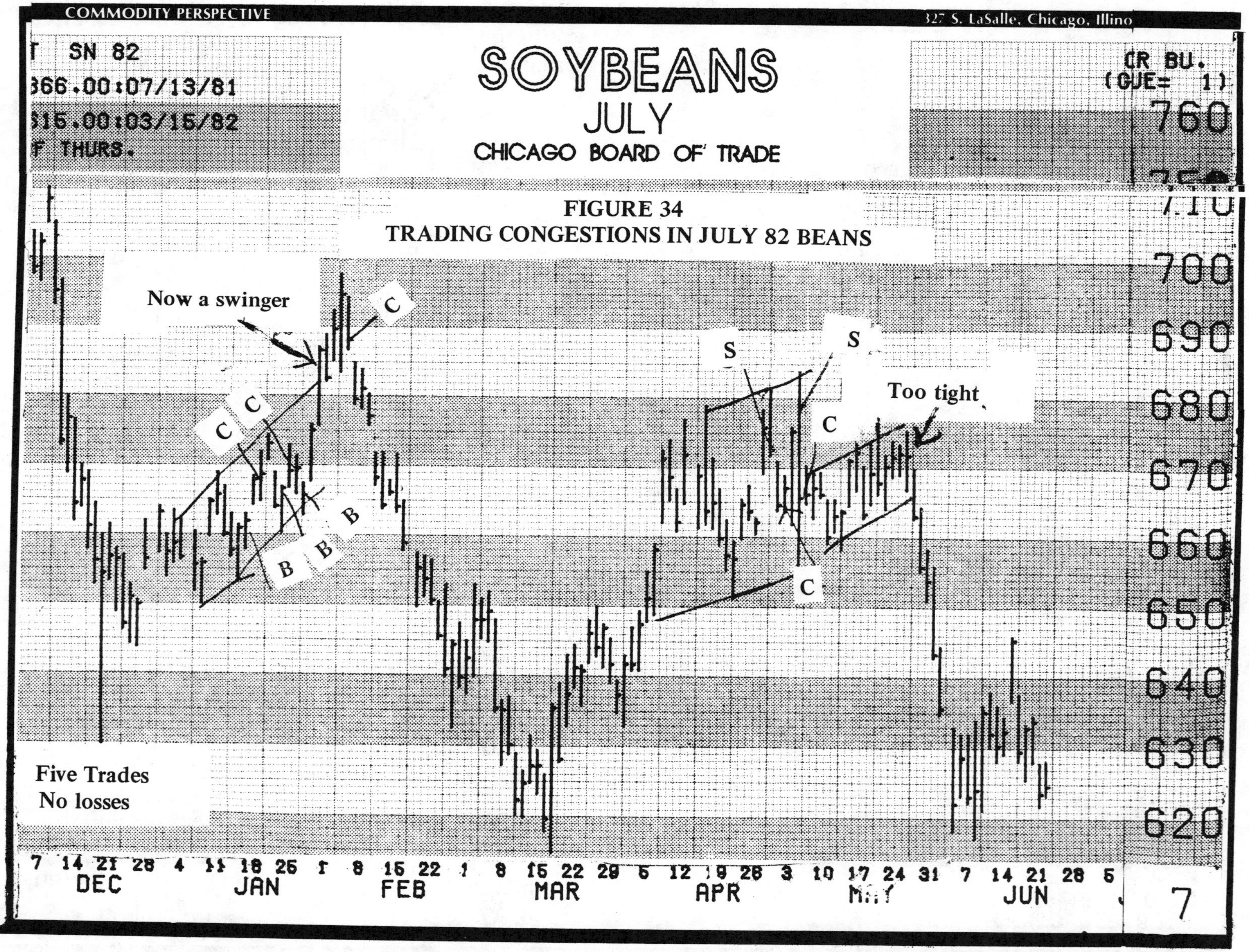

SOYBEANS
JULY
CHICAGO BOARD OF TRADE

FIGURE 34
TRADING CONGESTIONS IN JULY 82 BEANS

SN 82

366.00:07/13/81

$15.00:03/15/82

THURS.

dR BU.
(ONE= 1)

760

750

710

700

690

680

670

660

650

640

630

620

Now a swinger

Too tight

S

S

C

C

C

C

C

C

B

B

B

Five Trades
No losses

DEC   JAN   FEB   MAR   APR   MAY   JUN

7 14 21 28   4 11 18 26 1   8 16 22 1   8 15 22 29   5 12 19 28   3 10 17 24 31   7 14 21 28 5   7

327 S. LaSalle, Chicago, Illino

Chart furnished courtesy Commodity Perspective

82

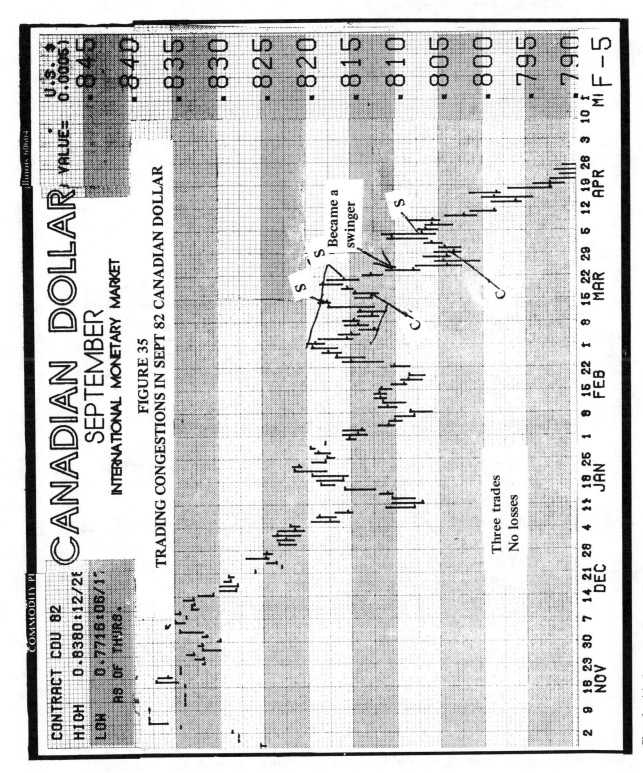

FIGURE 35

TRADING CONGESTIONS IN SEPT 82 CANADIAN DOLLAR

Three trades
No losses

SEPTEMBER 82 SWISS FRANC (See Figure 36)

Jump in on the 0-2 line, as it is with the trend, then reverse when the bottom line is hit. Price made a perfect retracement right where the 0-2 configuration signaled it would.

This was a broad-swinging congestion which made trading easier and was very profitable.

Five trades with no losses.

SEPTEMBER 82 CD (See Figure 37)

This is an interesting chart pattern. It went into what could be termed a channel or labored move. This made trading easier, but it was really a series of little congestions too small to have been traded by themselves had not the 0-2 line worked so beautifully.

Three trades with no losses.

OCTOBER 82 CATTLE (See Figure 38)

The first mark left you wondering. Was it or was it not a congestion?

After the second pivot is penetrated, wait for it to get within 25% of the bottom 0-2 line, then buy for a nice profit.

Finally, a channel was established, as well as the 0-2 lines, and you could sell as well as buy. The selling was only done after a close below two previous closes which was also still in the upper 25% of the 0-2 lines. Be very careful how you sell in these situations.

Five trades and no losses. These congestions do not make much at one time; but, done properly, they are some of the safest trades you can make.

SEPTEMBER 82 BRITISH POUND (See Figure 39)

The first 0-2 line was drawn for a trade on March 17. You must have an exit method that covers quickly, in case of a reversal. Penetration by the last two closes is all right, but I've known some traders to use the

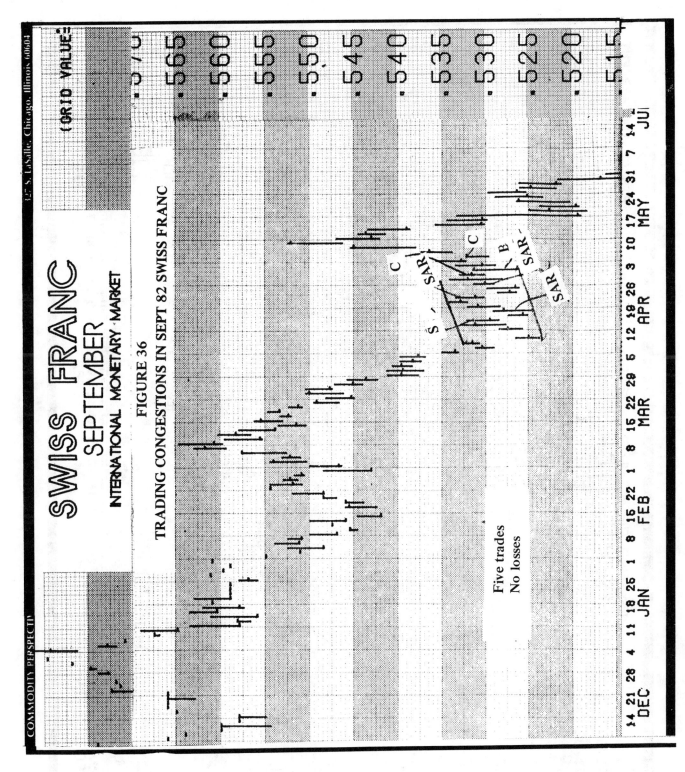

FIGURE 36

TRADING CONGESTIONS IN SEPT 82 SWISS FRANC

Five trades
No losses

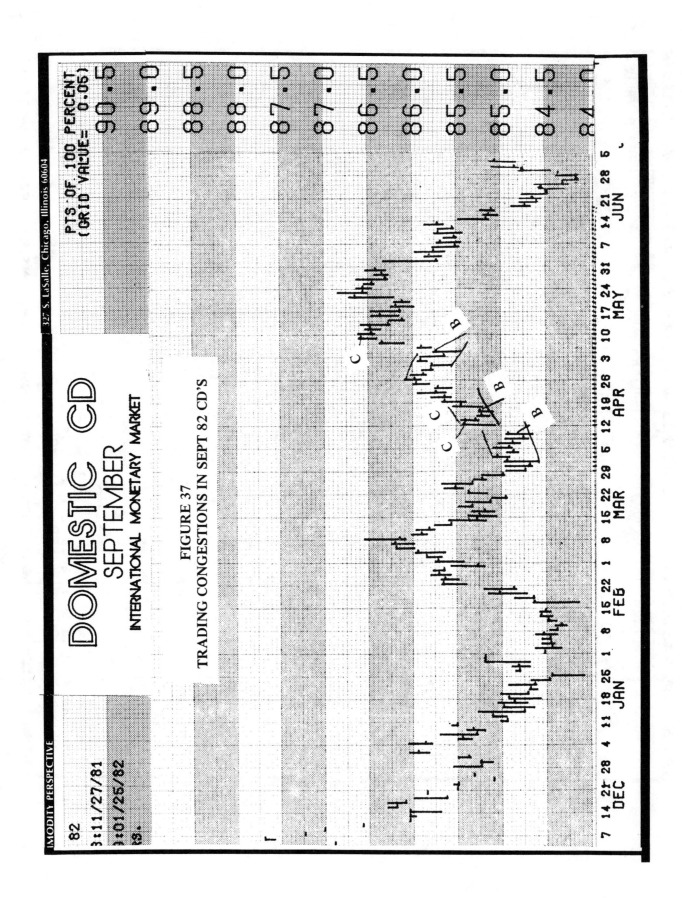

FIGURE 37
TRADING CONGESTIONS IN SEPT 82 CD'S

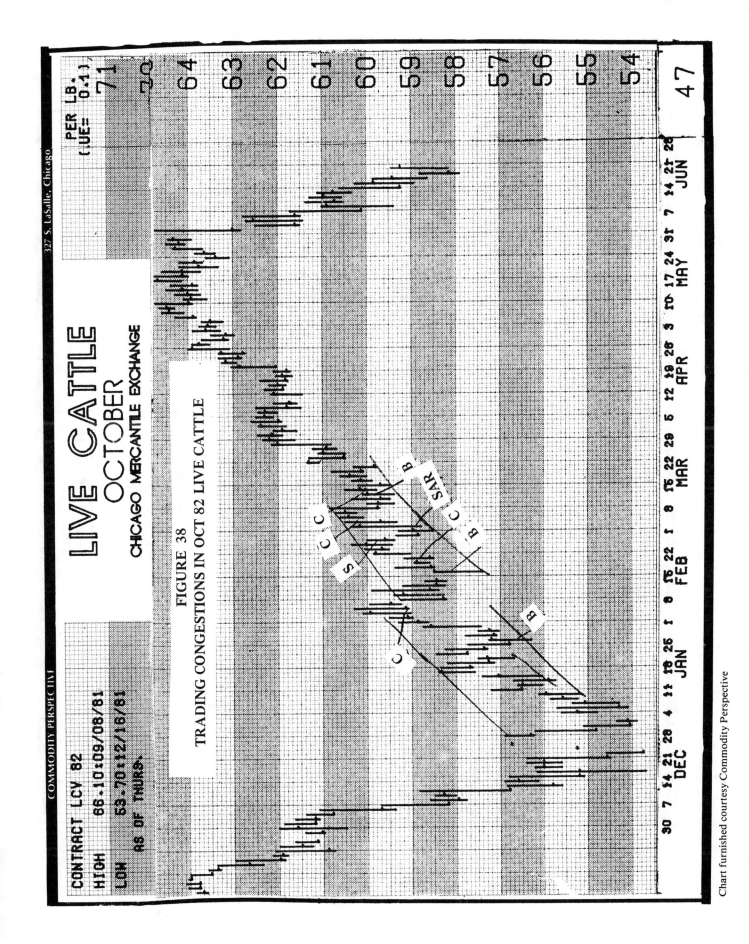

FIGURE 38
TRADING CONGESTIONS IN OCT 82 LIVE CATTLE

87

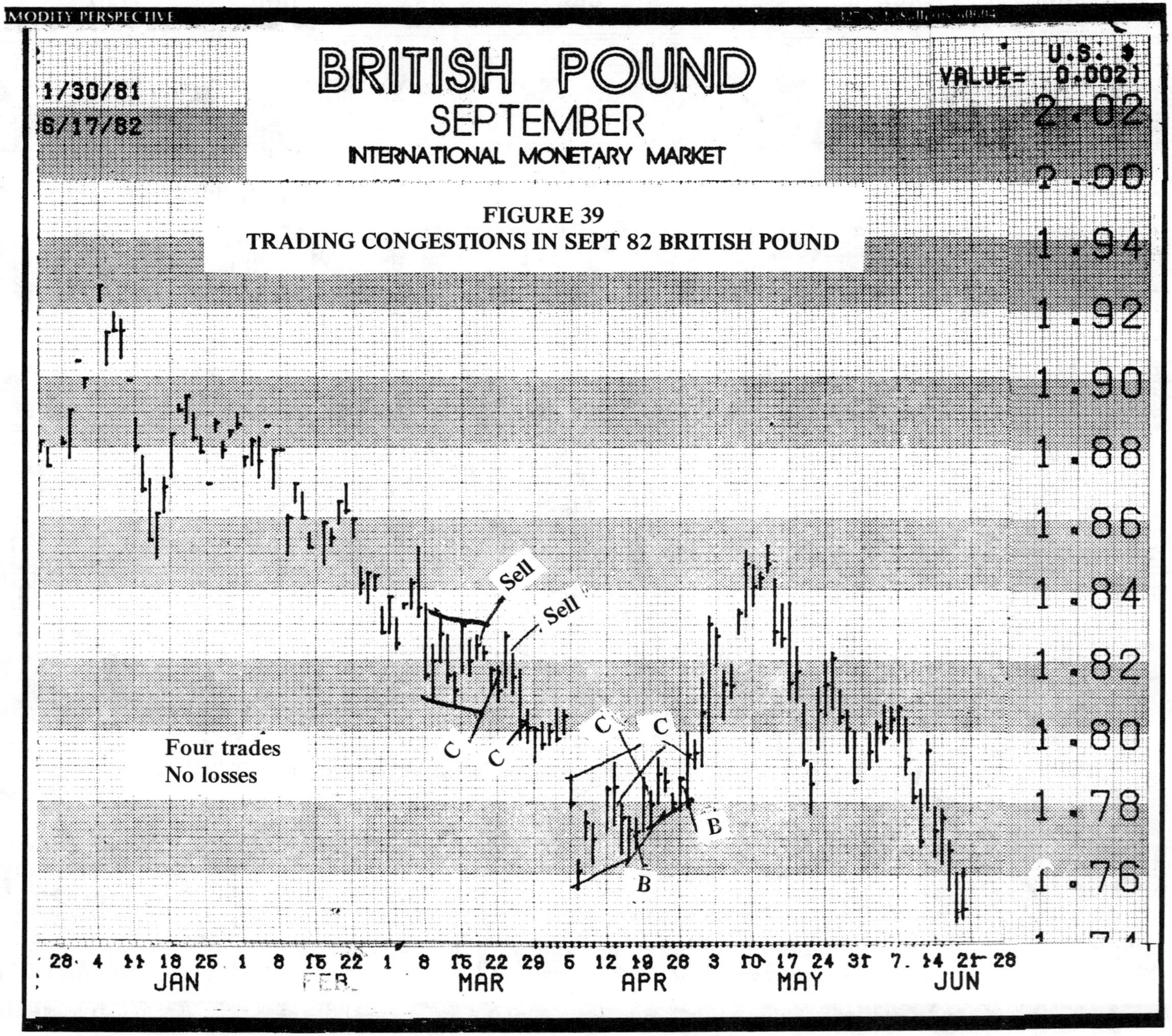

BRITISH POUND

SEPTEMBER
INTERNATIONAL MONETARY MARKET

VALUE = U.S. $ 0.0021

1/30/81
6/17/82

2.02
2.00
1.94
1.92
1.90
1.88
1.86
1.84
1.82
1.80
1.78
1.76

FIGURE 39

TRADING CONGESTIONS IN SEPT 82 BRITISH POUND

Sell
Sell II
C C C
C C C
B
B

Four trades
No losses

JAN   FEB   MAR   APR   MAY   JUN

Chart furnished courtesy Commodity Perspective

88

penetration of the previous high if short, or penetration of the previous day's low if long.

The bottom made an unusual turn, but as is the case 80% of the time, the 0-2 lines prove to be profitable even though breaking a trend.

There are four trades and no losses.

Chapter Six

Fast Fib Analysis

"THE BIG ONE THAT GOT AWAY" SHOULD NOT GET AWAY AGAIN

Reactions concern most traders, especially those who trade long term. With profits eroding, they wonder if the reaction may turn into a reversal of trend. This is why many traders try to use price projection analysis. Instead of merely hoping everything will be okay, they do something to estimate where to take profits. A lot of trading methods do need price projection analysis or profits will be lost and there will be the irritating occurrence of gains turning into losses.

Fast Fib analysis is good for price projection analysis, but should also become one of the best indicators you could use.

HOW FIB ANALYSIS WORKS

Fast Fib analysis estimates the distance of a reaction or counter trend, and how far a main swing should go, as well as when to expect a congestion to be over. The work here is mostly concerned with using proportional dividers, which are recommended for every trader. They save a lot of calculating time. It only takes a minute to set the dividers to obtain a lot of important information. Much more than swing size estimation may be learned with the use of Fib numbers and ratios. Traders who become good with this technique can make money in the markets even using nothing else.

I do not propose to teach anyone how to do long term price prediction, although some advisors use Fib ratios in an effort to do this. Later, I will give some of the formulas people use; but, for long term projection, I recommend the use of Balance Point Lines, Gravity Lines, or True Trend Lines. These are quicker and more reliable for predicting the long term trend. If the True Trend Line is broken, a long term trader should consider the trend changed for several months.

WAYS TO USE FIB NUMBERS AND RATIOS

There are several ways to use these ratios and Fib numbers. I will not explain all of them, but will cover those I feel are most important.

The chart in Figure 40 illustrates one of the easiest ways of using Fib numbers. Note that the Fib numbers are written along the downward path of market data. First, mark a ruler with the numbers scaled to the Commodity Perspective charts which are being used. Then lay the ruler along the path of the main trend of the market, starting with the top pivot on the numbers at the top of the channel. The bottom numbers should be started on the first pivot that occurs below the top pivot (used for the upside Fib numbers). If anyone were to lay a blank piece of paper over most of the data this would still predict the bottom within a cent, just knowing the location of only the first few pivots.

Most pivots in market price action will have a Fib number close by, unless there is topping or bottoming action such as that seen for number 55 (Figure 40), where price swings went below and above the number in equal distances, telling the trader that the end was coming soon. Here the Fib number was the gravity center point of the price swings below and above it. When a move that has been going for a long time starts making equal swings above and below the Fib number, expect the end of the move to occur very soon. Eventually, price will break away from one set of Fib numbers and start a new line of travel, requiring a new start on the numbering.

Spirals on Fib numbers are another way to obtain help with Fib ratios (see examples in Figures 41 and 42). The spirals are really circles, using the

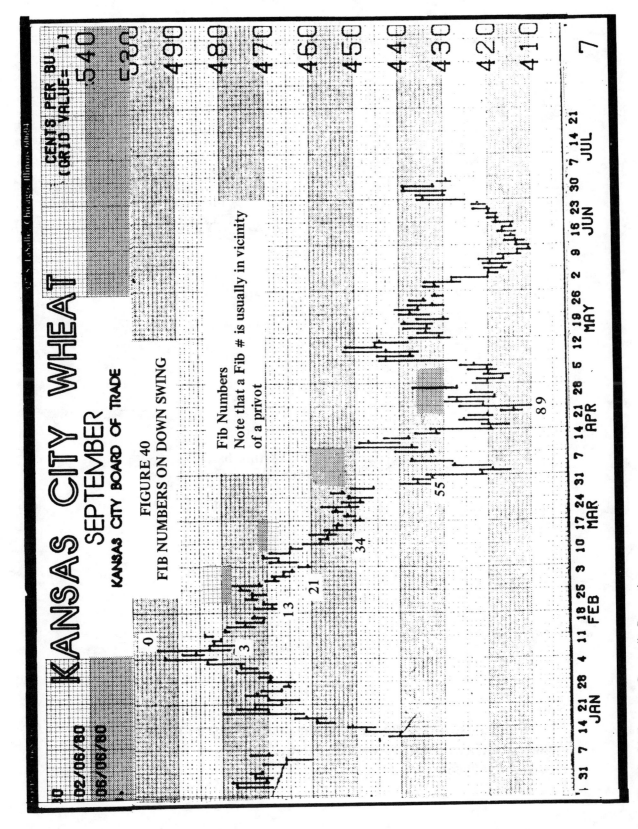

KANSAS CITY WHEAT
SEPTEMBER
KANSAS CITY BOARD OF TRADE

FIGURE 40
FIB NUMBERS ON DOWN SWING

Fib Numbers
Note that a Fib # is usually in vicinity
of a privot

FIGURE 41
ORION COMPUTER WORK ON SPIRALS

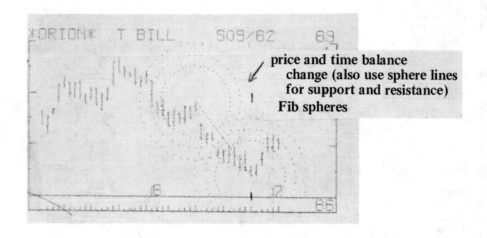

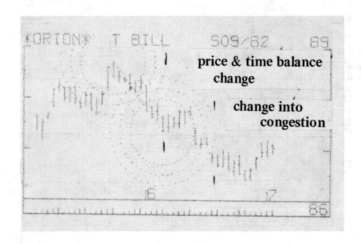

Note:

To obtain software for running the above program on an Apple II, contact **OMEGA MICROWARE, INC.**, 222 So. Riverside Plaza, Chicago, IL 60606

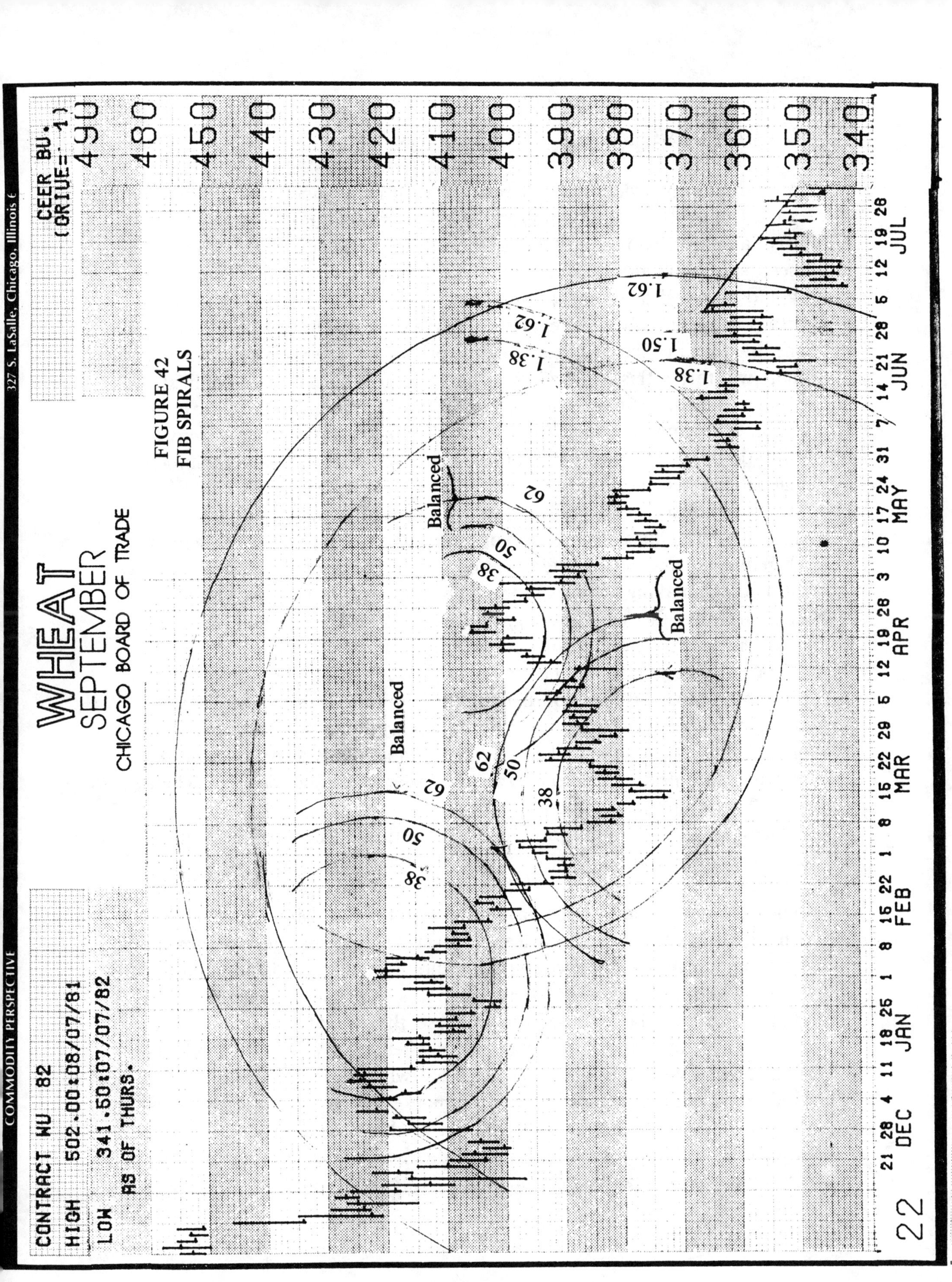

FIGURE 42
FIB SPIRALS

WHEAT
SEPTEMBER
CHICAGO BOARD OF TRADE

CONTRACT NU 82
HIGH   502.00±08/07/81
LOW   341.50±07/07/82
AS OF THURS.

CEER BU.
(ORIUE=¹)

COMMODITY PERSPECTIVE

327 S. LaSalle, Chicago, Illinois €

Chart furnished courtesy Commodity Perspective

95

range of a swing divided into Fib ratios as their radii. Find the length of the range from the top to the bottom of a swing, measure off thirty-eight, fifty, and sixty-two percent of it, then draw circles using the length of these, starting from either the top or the bottom of the swing. These lines should offer resistance or support. They also should help in balancing time with price, especially if the charts are made on a one to one basis, having one line for time and one equal line for price. Holes left for holidays on a chart will throw this off, and must be accounted for. More complicated detail may be done on the spirals by dividing the circumference of the circle to mark off equal spacing for Fib count. The proportional dividers may be set to do this quickly, and speed lines may be drawn to the main numbers that will intersect with price.

Speed lines are another way to use Fib ratios. The range is divided on a straight vertical line up from a top or bottom using Fib ratios of the length. Then lines are drawn from the top or bottom of the pivot through these Fib ratio points, making the lines proceed on expanding Fib ratios. This is not as accurate as other methods in giving support or resistance and should be used primarily for comparison with other indicators.

Time change points may be estimated with Fib ratios. Here, again, the range of the swing is used for dividing into Fib ratio length. These lengths are then measured from the top or bottom along the lines representing time on the graph. The line is marked off horizontally, but vertical lines must be drawn toward price action so they will be easier to see and interpret. There is an illustration of these in Figure 43 labeled Time Lines.

These are the four main ways to use Fib ratios. I will give several more later that will also help a lot.

Formulas and equations have been used by some analysts to calculate longer term predictions, but I have not found them to be much help for a commodity trader. Too much leeway must be used for the fast moving commodities. A price prediction with a month's variation is no good for anyone except millionaires, and even then it is bad to let the market move against you very far. Those who propose the use of these long term methods give illustrations with many inconsistencies. None of the methods have shown even a fifty percent accuracy when tested under unbiased conditions. The main thing is to let the market tell you what to do. This work only requires the last three swings to predict where the next swing or thrust will go. Fib ratios may be used on price action to give swing analysis, congestion analysis, and time change analysis.

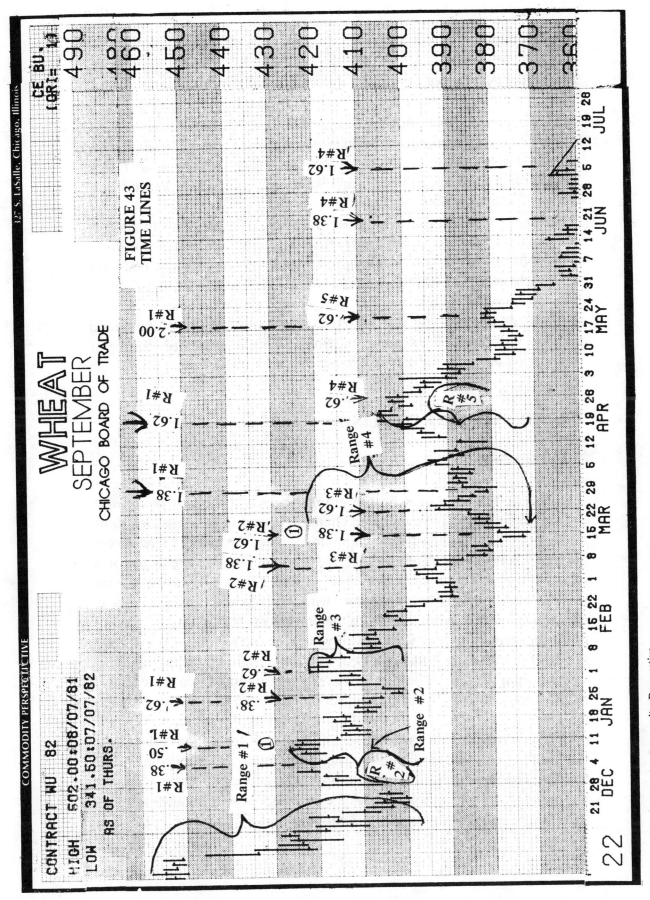

FIGURE 43
TIME LINES

Chart furnished courtesy Commodity Perspective

THE TESTING DONE

All markets do not behave the same. The system works better on some than on others. Optimizing may be done to help clarify what is working best in a market. I give a lot of guidelines below, letting you know what I have found that is most apt to be of help. Some skill is involved. Practice and study will usually make anyone better.

No log or semi-log charts have been used here. If you wish to get that involved, you will find that there are times the semi-log charts help. There is no apparent rule for determining in advance which will work best—the regular charting methods or semi-log. This makes it necessary to do both in order to see which is best.

As far as I know, there is no way to separate the use of Fibonacci without including Elliott wave methods. I have separated them for explanation only. They must go together in actual practice.

DRAWING THE FIB RATIO LINES

1. *Time Lines*

Horizonal Fib ratio lines on the graph represent time periods when a change is expected. The anticipated change of trend may be up, down, or sideways. See the dashed lines coming down from the marks going across the page in Figure 43. The distance is found by dividing the range of a swing into Fib ratio numbers of .62, .38 and .50. Notice where I have marked with brackets five different swings and labeled each. You may measure from the top down or from the bottom up, starting with the outer tip of the pivot and going vertically to where the top (or bottom) will be at the exact price where it had reversed. The thirty-eight will be at the top if starting from the top, or on the bottom when beginning from there. Label them so you will know what you did should you need to refer to them at a later date.

It is best to draw your own charts. The holes left for holidays throw off the lines by the space of the holes. The changing of scales by commercial charting companies will often cause problems and extra work. If you're not drawing your own charts, order the commercial ones by the month so there will be enough time to use the lines once they are drawn.

2. *The Price Lines*

The distance of the swing's range is found the same way it is found for Time Lines. Then the swing is marked into Fib ratio proportions, and lines are drawn horizontally across the page, so the price amount may be easily known when the line is intercepted by price (see Figure 44). If price is on a main trend downward, the longer lines for 1.38, 1.50, and 1.62 may be drawn by starting from the top and measuring down. The lines from different swings will come close to each other occasionally. Having several lines intercepting with price makes for a stronger support or resistance point.

3. *Speed Lines*

These are drawn like other Speed Lines, except they use Fib ratio angles instead of the thirds normally used (see Figure 45). Mark the Fib ratio points on the rise from the low, then bring the lines down from the top to each of them. These are best used as strength or weakness comparison lines. If price goes through a line, it is expected to continue to the next. The lines are primarily for each swing, and do not have much value if continued into the next swing.

4. *Spirals*

These are actually circles drawn on Fib ratio points at the distance of the divided range, as was done in the others techniques described above. The Fib ratio distance of the range becomes the radius of the circles (see Figure 42). These are called spirals because they are soon overlaid into each other to make a harmonious pattern. When time and price are scaled on a chart with a one-to-one ratio, these spirals may also show the balancing of time and price. Note from the illustration that a change comes when price runs out of the boundaries.

5. *Putting Them All Together*

Figure 46 shows all four of the Fib ratio lines drawn on one page, using the same high to low swing distance. The high on Dec. 2nd gives the price to use, and the low is on Mar. 16th. This is divided into 38%, 50%, & 62%.

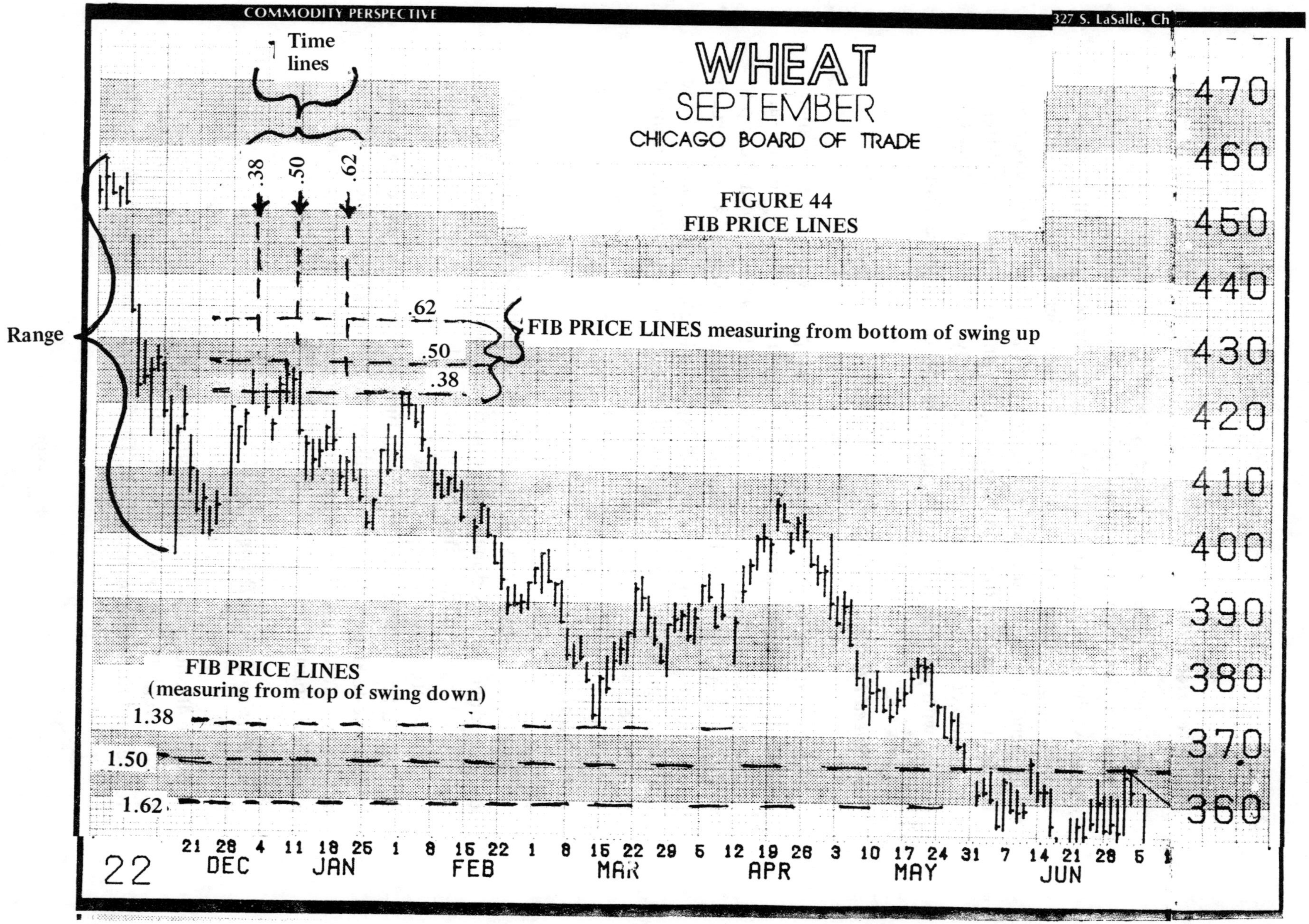

WHEAT
SEPTEMBER
CHICAGO BOARD OF TRADE

FIGURE 44
FIB PRICE LINES

327 S. LaSalle, Ch

FIB PRICE LINES measuring from bottom of swing up

Time lines

.62
.50
.38

.62
.50
.38

Range

FIB PRICE LINES
(measuring from top of swing down)

1.38
1.50
1.62

470
460
450
440
430
420
410
400
390
380
370.
360

22 21 28 4 11 18 25 1 8 15 22 1 8 15 22 29 5 12 19 28 3 10 17 24 31 7 14 21 28 5
    DEC   JAN   FEB   MAR   APR   MAY   JUN

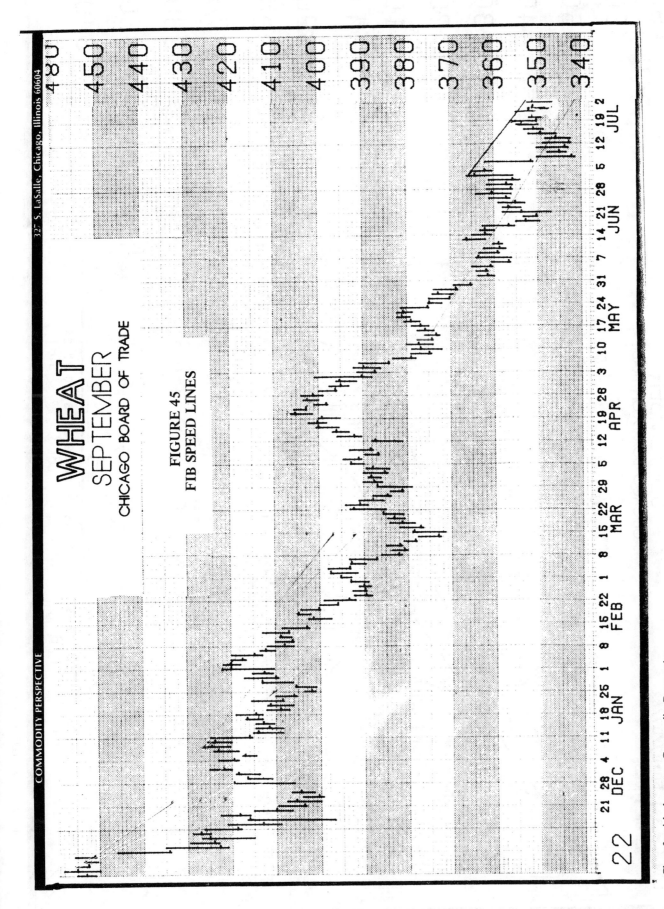

COMMODITY PERSPECTIVE

327 S. LaSalle, Chicago, Illinois 60604

WHEAT
SEPTEMBER
CHICAGO BOARD OF TRADE

FIGURE 45
FIB SPEED LINES

101

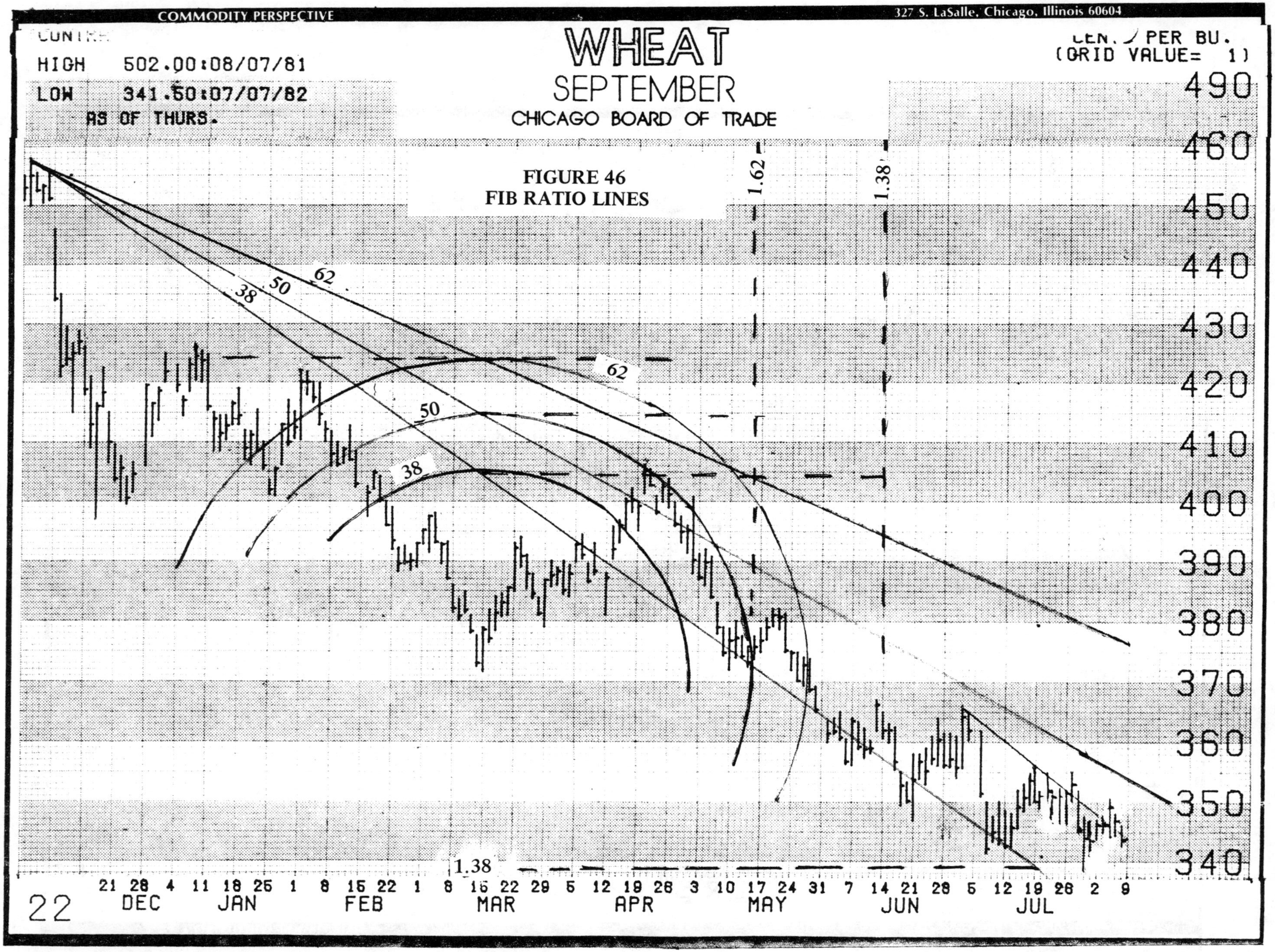

WHEAT
SEPTEMBER
CHICAGO BOARD OF TRADE

FIGURE 46
FIB RATIO LINES

COMMODITY PERSPECTIVE

327 S. LaSalle, Chicago, Illinois 60604

LEN. / PER BU.
(GRID VALUE= 1)

HIGH   502.00:08/07/81
LOW   341.50:07/07/82
AS OF THURS.

Chart furnished courtesy Commodity Perspective

102

Time lines are put out on 1.38 and 1.62 of the swing, starting at the high of Dec. 2nd.

WHERE THIS WILL WORK BEST

The first thing commodity traders want to know is what works best. It is not easy to answer this, because a lot of conditions will make a difference. Let me begin by telling you which kind of market is best suited for this work.

Swing markets or choppy markets have more pivots to use as references and are easier to use. The kind of market does make a difference; for example, a runaway market should not have more than a 38% reaction. A choppy market that has been going back to its old bottoms and tops will probably continue to do so until it breaks out into a different type of market. Long congestions usually have several false breakouts. Every price pattern needs to be studied individually to see how each works best in relation to these ratios.

Experience has shown the following commodities to only work on a long term basis: Sugar, Foreign Currencies, and Heating Oil.

Any thin market with small open interest and volume must allow a good "orb of tolerance," so you can expect the results to be under par. If the above mentioned commodities become choppy, the results should be even better!

Markets moving very smoothly need to be scaled to accentuate the swings.

Weekly charts may be used, but these instructions are based on dailies. Changing from the dailies to weeklies, or to intra-day data, requires a different perspective. A breakout on one may not be a breakout on the other. The time difference must be kept in mind, so that day trading periods are not used as daily time periods, and that daily work is not used as weekly, unless they both happen to come to the same price level.

WHAT WORKS BEST

The best condition is one where several Fib lines or ratio points are in the same area merging with price. Price swing work needs to be done from the reactions upward or downward, and also from the last swing. There are six easy-to-do Fib estimation methods, and at least three of them should agree if using all six. Cutting out the speed lines, which are rather weak in predictive ability, would leave five. There are two swing projection techniques, the Time lines, The Price lines, and the Spiral, making five in all. The spirals are best for balancing, so this leaves four that are most important for predicting. If two of these four agree, you have a good indicator. More about this later, but first I'll show you how to make the swing predictions.

1. *Swing Predictions*

Use the large side of the dividers to start, set on the 62% mark. Open them wide enough to cover the distance of three pivots. Switch to the opposite side and put a point down where the last pivot ended. The other point of the dividers should come close to where the next pivot will be.

Next take the large side of the dividers and measure the previous price swing from bottom to top. Turn the dividers over and measure from the last pivot. This should find the end of the next swing, as the dividers were set on the .62 mark and this is 62% of the swing measured (see Figure 47).

The third way is to measure the last reaction or correction with the small side of the dividers still set on the 62% mark. Turn this over and go from the low, (or high) of the reaction to help find the next pivot.

2. *Finding The End Of A Congestion*

Put the large side of the dividers, set on .62 mark, over the last two congestion areas, then place the other side down where the new congestion area seems to be forming. This works quite often.

The distance across the last congestion, using the small side of the dividers, will also often find the end of the next congestion by putting the large side at the beginning of a suspected congestion. Figures 48 and 49 are illustrations of this.

Use both price and time measurements to help find pivots and congestion endings. The ratios work on time as well as price.

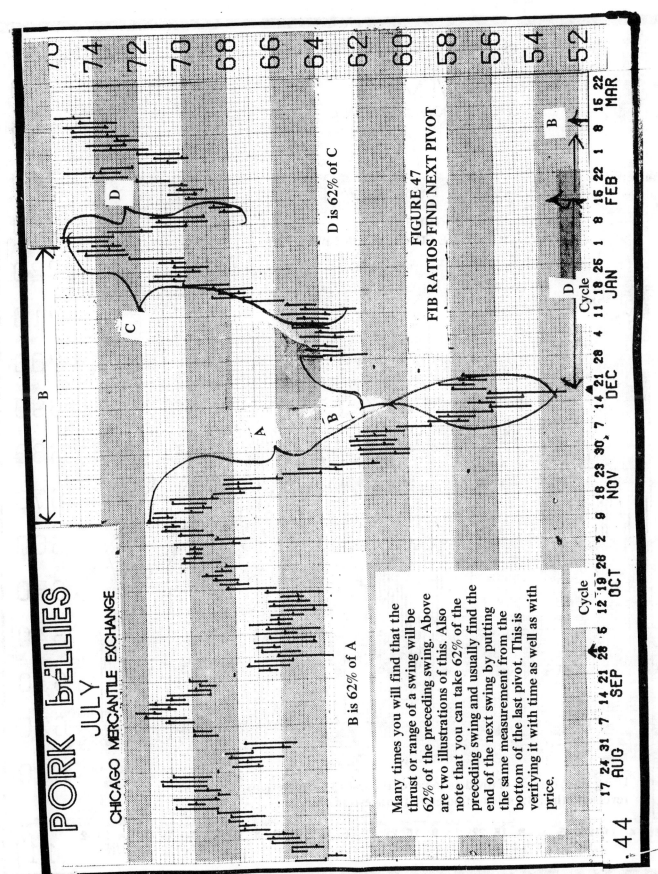

PORK BELLIES
JULY
CHICAGO MERCANTILE EXCHANGE

B is 62% of A

D is 62% of C

Many times you will find that the thrust or range of a swing will be 62% of the preceding swing. Above are two illustrations of this. Also note that you can take 62% of the preceding swing and usually find the end of the next swing by putting the same measurement from the bottom of the last pivot. This is verifying it with time as well as with price.

FIGURE 47
FIB RATIOS FIND NEXT PIVOT

105

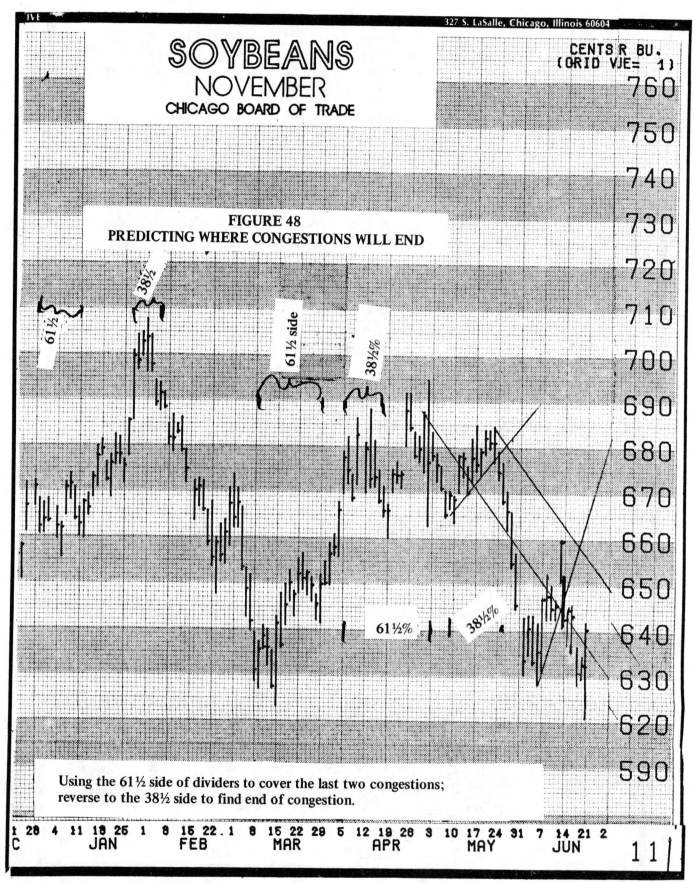

FIGURE 48
PREDICTING WHERE CONGESTIONS WILL END

Using the 61½ side of dividers to cover the last two congestions;
reverse to the 38½ side to find end of congestion.

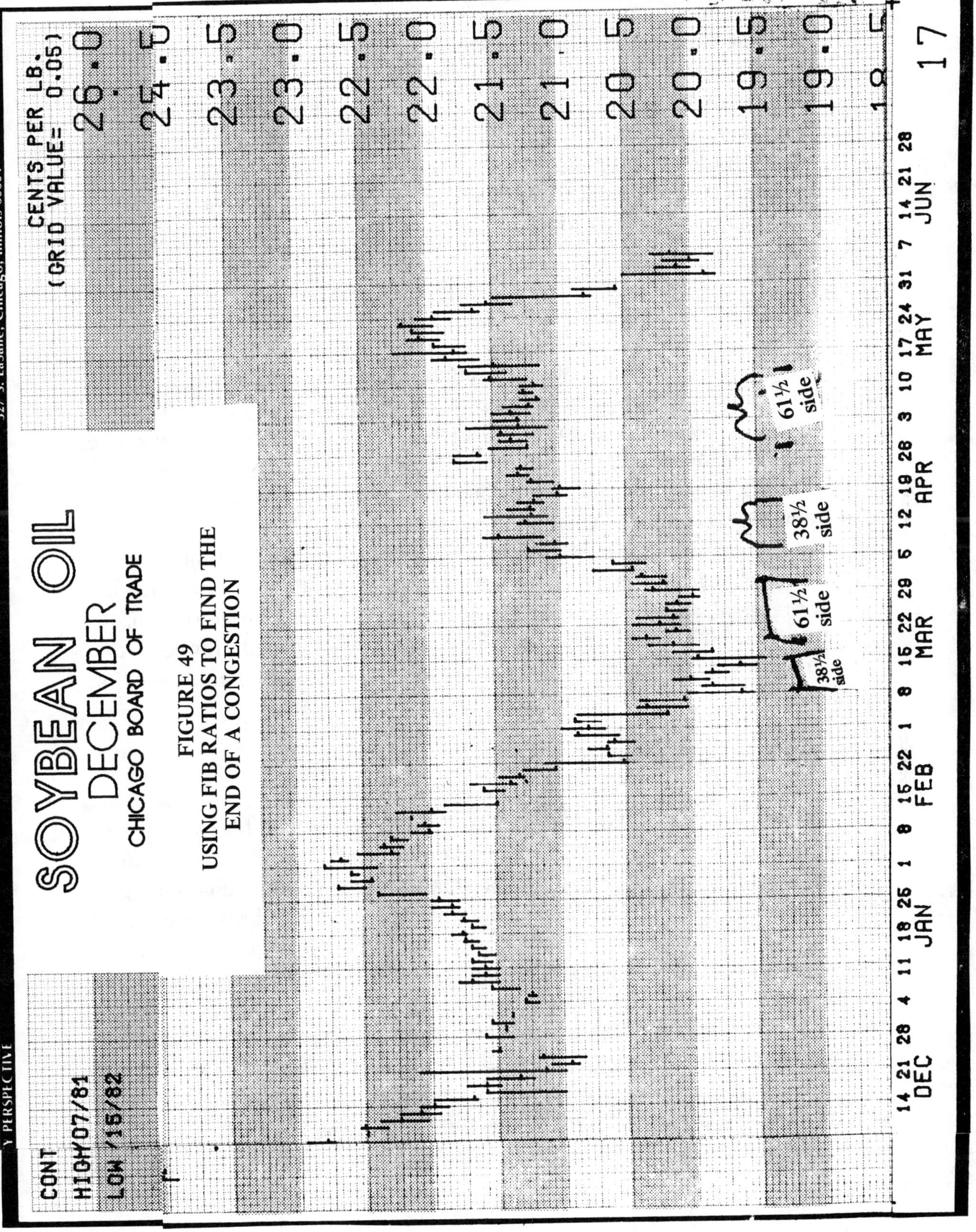

SOYBEAN OIL

DECEMBER
CHICAGO BOARD OF TRADE

FIGURE 49
**USING FIB RATIOS TO FIND THE
END OF A CONGESTION**

CONT
HIGH 07/81
LOW 16/82

CENTS PER LB.
(GRID VALUE= 0.05)

26.0
25.0
23.5
23.0
22.5
22.0
21.5
21.0
20.5
20.0
19.5
19.0

61½
side

38½
side

61½
side

38½
side

14 21 28 | 4 11 18 25 | 1 8 15 22 | 1 8 15 22 29 | 5 12 19 28 | 3 10 17 24 31 | 7 14 21 28 | 17
DEC | JAN | FEB | MAR | APR | MAY | JUN

Chart furnished courtesy Commodity Perspective

107

3. *Time Ratios Between Pivot Tops And Bottoms*

The distance between two pivots, measured with the dividers set on the 62 mark using the large side, will often find the next pivot when the other side of the dividers is placed on the tip of the last pivot. In some cases this distance will find several pivots in a row, since price action makes efforts to change in equal time periods or cycles. See the illustration of this in Figure 47.

4. *Be Consistent*

There will never be consistent winnings unless the trader makes definite trading rules to follow and sticks by them religiously until they are proved unworthy. Some Fib ratio users start from a bottom of a reaction one time, then from the top of the reaction the next, apparently doing anything to make it work on past data. Changing the rules during a test is invalid unless complete new testing is done. Some testing and optimizing is needed; but once the course of action is set the rules and definitions must not be changed. Eventually, you do run out of a ratio's area of influence for reversal, and new lines and ratios must be found. It is necessary for the trader to have specific rules and reasons set down and followed. Don't change in the middle of a trade unless your rules substantiate that the time is right.

5. *What Doesn't Work*

There is an old formula that has been whispered around for twenty years. It takes the range of the first wave of a move and multiplies this by 3.618, then adds this to the price of the bottom of wave one to predict the top of the third thrust. Half of this added to the top of the first thrust is supposed to find the top of the second thrust. If the market is going down, you subtract instead of adding. This method or formula has not worked! So ignore it.

Some "advisors" try to take 2 .618 times the range of a swing added to the bottom of the swing to predict the top of the second. It is true that 2.618 is the ratio of the second Fib number back, but relating this to market action does not work. Avoid this system also.

Some use two swings and their reactions, when one of the swings has a 38% retracement and the other 62%, to predict a big swing coming next. This is found so seldom it is hard to check for reliability. Perhaps eventually I will program this into the computer, but for now I have only found a very few cases to go by. These did work, however.

Robert Beckman, in his book *Supertiming*, indicated that he did not think the long term Fib formulas worked enough to be of value. We asked several other Fib experts and they agreed.

It is best to have a number of the Fib lines or Ratio reversal points agree on a price prediction.

WHAT TO COUNT ON TO BE DEPENDABLE

1. A swing retracement usually goes from 38% to 62% of the preceding swing, if you are not in a choppy sideways market.

2. In a zigzag swinging market, the wave after the correction is often 1.618 times the correction.

3. If a correction is weaker than expected, the next thrust should be stronger. Failures often tell more about the market than anything else.

4. Corrective waves are related to the previous number of the Fib series.

5. Main thrust waves relate to the higher number of the series.

6. The range of a congestion can generally be used the same as other reactions in a move to get the extent of the next move.

7. Corrections to main thrusts that follow the "A," "B," "C" pattern usually are more reliable on estimations. The "C" is generally about the same as the "A," but you must expect a much greater variety in the main thrusts. A good knowledge of the kinds of price patterns and of the use of the Elliott wave is important in becoming accurate with estimations.

Apparently, there are some big money people who believe in these ratios, especially for the trading of gold and silver, because I have noticed these commodities often turn right on the dime where the ratio projection is predicted. My advice is that you learn to do your own work and check these until you know for yourself. I believe it is possible to become good enough at this to make money using only these techniques.

HOW PRICE PATTERNS AFFECT THE FIB RATIOS

The momentum and volatility of the market makes a difference in how the ratio works. Expect a slow market to only have 38% reactions. This is where there is not enough steam to pressure the market very high on a rally. On the other hand, if a market is falling (or rising) much faster than usual, this should not have much of a rally or reaction either because there is too much strength in the move; especially for the first two legs of the market. Look for lack of pressure or too much pressure while learning to apply the Fib ratios.

Choppy markets and congestions are usually to be used as one unit. Measure the range of these for use, but do not try to predict where they will go until your work indicates the end. Most of the time it is back to base, run the stops, then up to the tops to get ready for another downward move. If there are not enough traders on board at the tops or bottoms of these choppy areas, then the pullback will only be about halfway, with another chance for more traders to get aboard. It is important here to watch volume and open interest. If there is a large rise in participation (of at least thirty and even better fifty percent more than usual) this could be a true breakout and not just floor traders having fun. Look for a sharp upturn in the open interest line and about twice the usual amount of volume for a day or two.

Swinging markets are more likely to have a 62% retracement. If the market starts out with a 62% reaction, expect this to continue for most others reactions in the move. The labored move is classified with the swinging move since, once price breaks out of the labored move's channel, it usually results in a fast swing.

USING ELLIOTT WAVE THEORY

The way a market gets started from its main lows is very important and must be kept in mind by the trader using Fib ratios and numbers. If it starts off with a five, three, five type of movement this should be a zigzag type of Elliott formation of the text book Elliott pattern. On the other hand, if the beginning of a move has a three, three, five pivot count in its up and down waves, this is more apt to be an Elliott flat or irregular market. The flats are a lot more choppy, and the irregulars have no clearly defined top or bottom line that can be used for trend indications.

It is important to know and remember the number of waves and the size of the waves that come off a bottom. On the size of waves there are several things to expect:

1. If there have been five small waves, expect the next to be larger.
2. When two legs of a move have only a 38% reaction, expect the next correction to be larger.
3. The third wave of Elliott count is expected to be larger than the first and usually larger than the fifth.

The angle of travel should be noticed too. Wave five is usually on the same angle as wave one, and not the same as the number three wave.

4. There are usually extensions in only one of the waves and not more than two.
5. Large triangles are in the fourth wave, ordinarily.
6. The fifth wave should be about the same size as the first, if there are no extensions.
7. Observe the rule of alternates. One out of the three main thrusts should be different both in length and angle of travel. If it happens that the first two are about the same, expect the third thrust to be greatly different.
8. A reversal is deemed to have begun when a corrective wave goes below the wave it is correcting; or if in a down market, above the wave it is correcting.
9. Learn to identify the Elliott "orthodox" top. This occurs on the fifth wave in Elliott count. An example was the Dow Jones Ind. Average High of 1928 before the irregular top in 1929. This is also called an Elliott "stacked top." I've discussed this formation previously, calling it the "three spears top." The reverse of this is an "orthodox" bottom where the count runs out, then a stacked bottom is formed with three points showing close together (along with long range days, usually).

(On the apparent contradiction between 8 and 9 above, the difference is the stack of three small waves making three points on the top or bottom).

LEARN AND REAP THE REWARDS

There should not be much time spent on making these lines because they extend out the full length of a swing and are usually good for a long time.

111

It does take some practice and study to become efficient at doing this. The rules and explanations given above should be all that is needed to make this one of the most important and fruitful techniques to use. Using the dividers makes it simple and quick. I have indicated the strategies that tested well. Some optimizing will help, but as skill is gained much of this may be eliminated. This is the type of thing that separates the serious trader from those who just want to take a shot in the dark.

SUGGESTED TRADING RULES USING FIB RATIOS

1. *General Rules*

a. A pivot must be a change from the previous line of travel, having at least two days of reversal. If there is a three day reversal close by, use this in preference to the two day.

b. Use a stop when entering. We suggest a six cent stop in grains.

c. Use an orb of tolerance for penetration of the lines. For example, in grains the lines must be penetrated by at least two cents. This order should be on-close-only.

d. Take profits one cent before the target area to make sure of fills.

e. The main idea of this trading method is to have several Fib numbers, ratio lines, or estimated turning points occur in one area. When this happens a trade is initiated. If price does not reach here, this is a failure and a trade going with the direction of the failure should be taken. If price goes easily through the support or resistance area, this is a trade signal.

2. *Specific Rules*

a. Use five or six of the Fib reversal methods, as explained earlier. Trade when price comes into an area where three or more of these signal a reversal.

b. Put your stop two cents beyond the other side of the reversal area.

c. Take profits when the next smallest Fib ratio line or reversal point is reached.

d. Always abort the trade when price closes beyond the last four previous closes.

THE POTENTIAL OF THIS
FIB RATIO WORK IS EXCITING

I have found a variation of the above rules that appears so far to be quite successful. It will take a lot of time and money to give this the testing necessary to know for sure if it really works; but I intend to do this, and may, some day, have something to offer as a result of these more extensive tests.

REFERENCE

Those who want to learn more about Elliott and Fib ratio theory should buy *Supertiming* by Robert C. Beckman, The Library of Investment Study, P. O. Box 25177, Los Angeles, CA 90025.

A FAST FIB TRADING METHOD

I. *Definitions*

1. Pivot—There must be three days going in one direction, then at least two days of reversal in the opposite direction. It is better if there are three days of reversal; so use the three days if one is close by since this is more significant. A two day reversal is better than none, however. When price goes beyond the last eight days of closes before the last change of direction, this is also a pivot. (This accounts for congestions, where trading may be sideways before making a change).
2. Rallies are temporary changes of direction in a bear market.
3. Reactions are temporary changes of direction in a bull market.
4. Divider settings—The 62% mark is used, making 38% on the small

side and 62% on the large. Measuring with the small gives 1.62 on the large. We refer to the small side as 38% and the large as 62%.

5. Stoploss—6 cents in grains, more in others according to volatility.

II. *General Rules*

A. Change of Trend
1. There must be a three day change pivot followed by a three day reaction.
2. The trend is changed when any pivot is surpassed.

B. When to Buy or Sell
1. When the target is reached, you exit or bring the stops up very close. When the trend line is crossed in the opposite direction, reverse with this crossing. Two estimations for the price target must be done; one by using 62% of the previous swing, and one by using 1.62 of the last reaction or rally.

    If the estimation of the smallest projection does not show six cents in grains, do not trade.

    To measure the range of a rally or reaction, use the small side of the dividers, then reverse for getting the estimation. The high to low swing is measured with the large side and reversed to the small side for the estimation of the target. It is in the opposite direction of the last swing or reaction.

    Make new projections each time the trend line is broken.

    Measure using the distance from the high to the low on a vertical, rather than the peak to low from pivot tops.

C. Exiting or Taking Profits
1. You exit when the stop loss is hit.
2. Use the smallest of the two estimations for the target to be on the safe side, then get out one cent early as additional protection against bad fills.

LEGEND

1. A number like "2" with an "S" and either "T" or "B" at a line

means this is the swing number; "T" stands for "top," and "B" means bottom. This shows where measurements were made with the large side of the dividers on the last main swing.

2. A number followed by "R" along with a "T" or "B" means a rally or reaction line for the high and low of this short reversal. These marks are where the small side of the dividers are used to measure, then reverse for an estimation.

3. "B" means buy.

4. "S" means sell.

February Trade By Trade Description of September 1982 Wheat (see Figure 50).

Start at December 1st on the left side of the graph. Price came down to make a low of 397, for a 61¢ move (ls). Going to the three day rally between December 9th and 11th, you find a 14¢ move (lr). 14 x 1.618 gives 22¢. This is smaller than the 37¢, so we add this to 400, making our target 422.

On January 8th, it appears that the rally is over and the main trend is still down, so we make a downside estimation. The range of this last swing from high to low was from (low on December 16th and high on January 7th) 426 to 397, or a 29¢ rise (2s). Expecting a main swing down, (2r) multiply 29 x 1.618, giving 46¢. Subtracting 46 from 426 makes our main target 380. Between December 31st and January 5th there was a ten cent reaction, 10 x 1.618 = 16¢ (2r). 16 from 426 gives our target of 410, since this is the smallest. There is a four day rally covering 11½¢. 11.5 x 1.618 gives 18¢ for the projected next drop, 18 from 419 is 401. This was exactly where price went. You need to make the trades M.I.T. (market if touched); and, (as stated in the rules), drop off one cent to make sure of a fill.

The low of 401 subtracted from the high of 426 on January 25th leaves 25 x .618 = 15, or a reaction upside target of 416 (3s). Going off the high of January 18th at 419 down to the low of 401 on January 25th, there is an 18¢ range, 18 x .618 is 11¢ + 401 = 412 target. Price went to 422.

On the next estimated target, subtract the high on February 1st at 422 from the low on January 25th at 401, leaving 21 x 1.618 (trend is still down). This equals 33¢, which is subtracted from 422 giving 389 (4r). The little two day stall from January 27 to February 1st has 8¢ x 1.618 = 12¢.

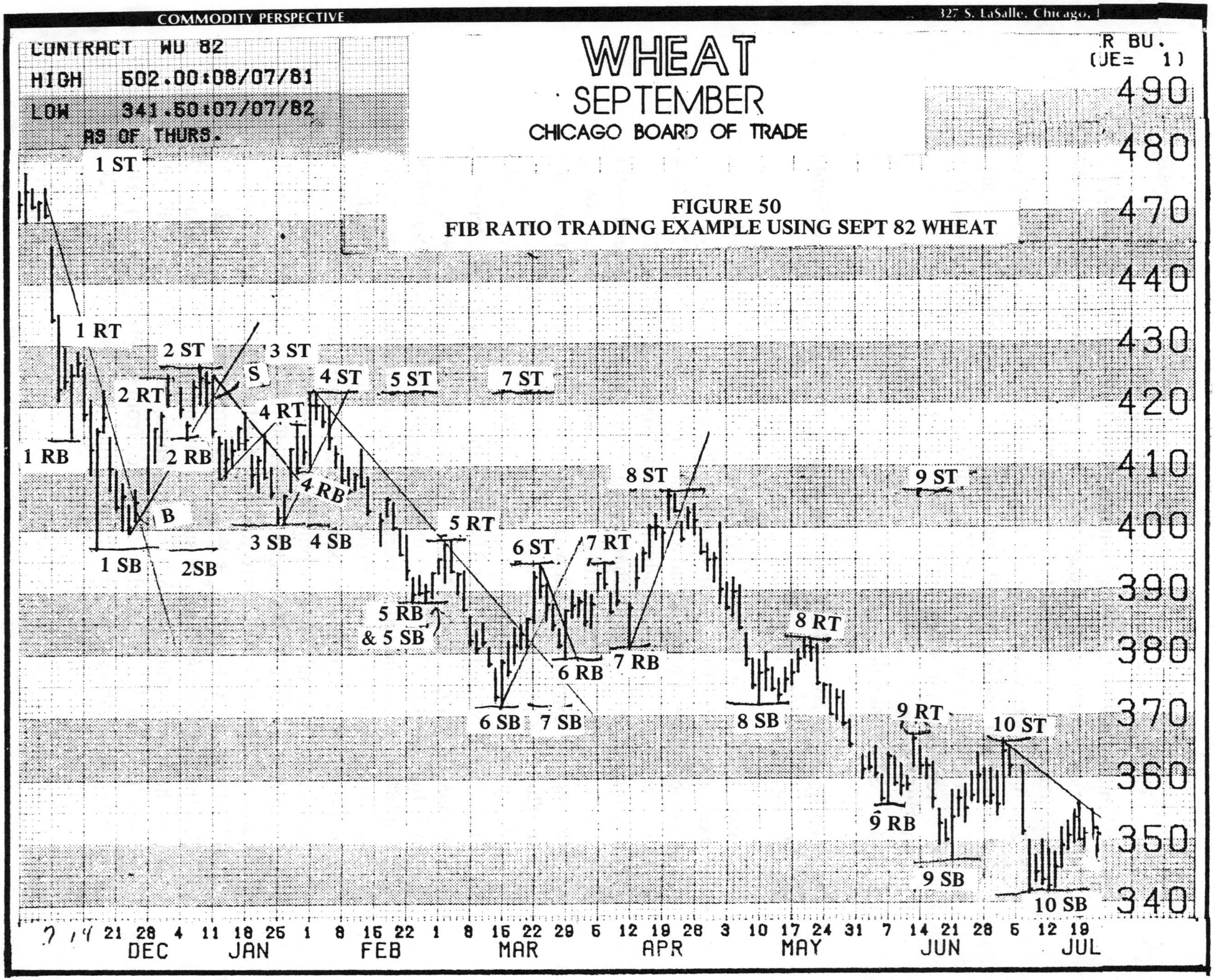
COMMODITY PERSPECTIVE
327 S. LaSalle, Chicago, I
CONTRACT WU 82
HIGH 502.00:08/07/81
LOW 341.50:07/07/82
AS OF THURS.
WHEAT
SEPTEMBER
CHICAGO BOARD OF TRADE
R BU.
(JE= 1)
490
480
470
440
430
420
410
400
390
380
370
360
350
340
1 ST
1 RT
1 RB
1 SB
B
2 ST
2 RT
2 RB
2SB
3 ST
S
3 SB
4 ST
4 RT
4 RB
4 SB
5 ST
5 RT
5 RB
& 5 SB
6 ST
6 SB
6 RB
7 ST
7 RT
7 RB
7 SB
8 ST
8 RT
8 SB
9 ST
9 RT
9 RB
9 SB
10 ST
10 SB
21 28 4 11 18 25 1 8 15 22 1 8 15 22 29 5 12 19 26 3 10 17 24 31 7 14 21 28 5 12 19
DEC JAN FEB MAR APR MAY JUN JUL

FIGURE 50
FIB RATIO TRADING EXAMPLE USING SEPT 82 WHEAT

Chart furnished courtesy Commodity Perspective

Subtracted from 422 this yields 410. Since the next little congestion did not have two days in a row going against you, it is okay to stay in for the longer target of 389. Each of the three little rallies projected the next small one down until it met our 389 target.

You are out at 389 and looking for a trade. The rally from 388 on February 23 to its high on March 2 is 8¢ x 1.618 = 12¢ (5r). 393 − 12 = 381. From the high of February 1 to the low of February 23 at 388 is 34¢ × .618 = 21¢; 398 − 21 = 377, our other projected low (5s). You must use 381, although 377 would have turned out to be better.

There has been a "five small number Elliott Pivot count" here, so expect a larger reaction. 62% of the previous swing puts the target at 389. 1.62 of the last 8¢ reaction mentioned above is 12¢ + 371 = 383, which isn't enough to trade. From the high of February 1 to the low of March 15 is 50¢ x .618, or 31¢. Added to the low of March 15 (of 372) gives an estimation of 402 (7s).

From the low on March 15 to the high on March 23 is 23¢ × .618 = 14¢; 394 − 14 = target of 380 (7s). There is no reaction to use within range. Using time to help, go from the high of February 1 to the high of March 2 with the 62% side of the dividers. Turn the other side down at the March 2 high and roll over. This hits the high of March 22 right on target. Go from the high of March 2 to the high of March 23, turn the dividers over and, starting from the high of March 23, you have the projected "time line" high on April 5 that proved to be only 2¢ off (6r). 1.62 x reaction of 15¢ between March 23 and March 29 is 24¢ estimated gain. This makes 403 your estimation. Expect a 14¢ reaction starting April 6, because it is 62% of the previous thrust or main swing, and it is on the time line described above. It is interesting here that even though there was a 14¢ reaction, there was not a close below the last four closes.

Now take the small side of the dividers to measure this last 14¢ reaction, then turn over the dividers and put one point on the bottom of April 12, or multiply 14 x 1.618 and add this to 381, giving 403, (7r), which is close enough for anyone.

The rules of action-reaction state that a gap should be used like a pivot. So measure up from the low of March 15 to the high of April 6 with the large side of the dividers, or multiply .618 x 24 getting 15. Go from the gap at 389 and add 15¢, making 404, as the second estimated target price (8s).

A third price is the time line. Take the space between the last three pivot highs; first is March 3 and last is April 6; now turn the dividers over to the small side and place one point on the last high of April 6. This gives you the perfect day to go short for a good trip down.

Take the high of April 20 and use the large divider side to measure down to the lowest low of the last swing at 371¢, March 15. This 36¢ x 1.618 gives a 58¢ estimated target for the next swing, or down to 349¢ (8r). Using the other methods would put you out at 385. So if it's not a long term trade, just measure the reactions with the short side to get close. The first leg could have been found by going from gap to top with the 62% side. Also, 1.62 from the top down gives 375 which is very close to the bottom.

Now you have five pivots down on this leg, so expect a bigger reaction. Also, there are failures here on the ratio projections, which signals that a congestion is coming.

Don't get discouraged. This may seem complicated the first time you read it. But it's really not too bad. You may want to reread this section—slowly. Keep referring to the chart, go step-by-step, and it will all become clear to you.

Chapter Seven

Improving Your Charting Ability

THE DOUBLE CHARTING TECHNIQUE

A good way to make a chart do double work is to take the daily charts and draw lines across the weekly highs and lows, blocking off this five day action in heavier lines, which emphasize the weekly highs and lows (see Figure 51).

There are two ways to make the weekly lines on the daily charts. A square line with a block type and a square line with an envelope type will do the same thing in a different manner. Since five lines on the dailies represents a week, marking straight across at the high and low makes these five lines represent the smaller one day line. The square block method is easier for us to interpret, so we prefer its use.

DRAWING THE DOUBLE CHART LINES

The daily graph marks should not be touched when drawing the weekly blocks or their value may be diminished. It is also better to use different colored pens to clearly set the weeklies off from the dailies.

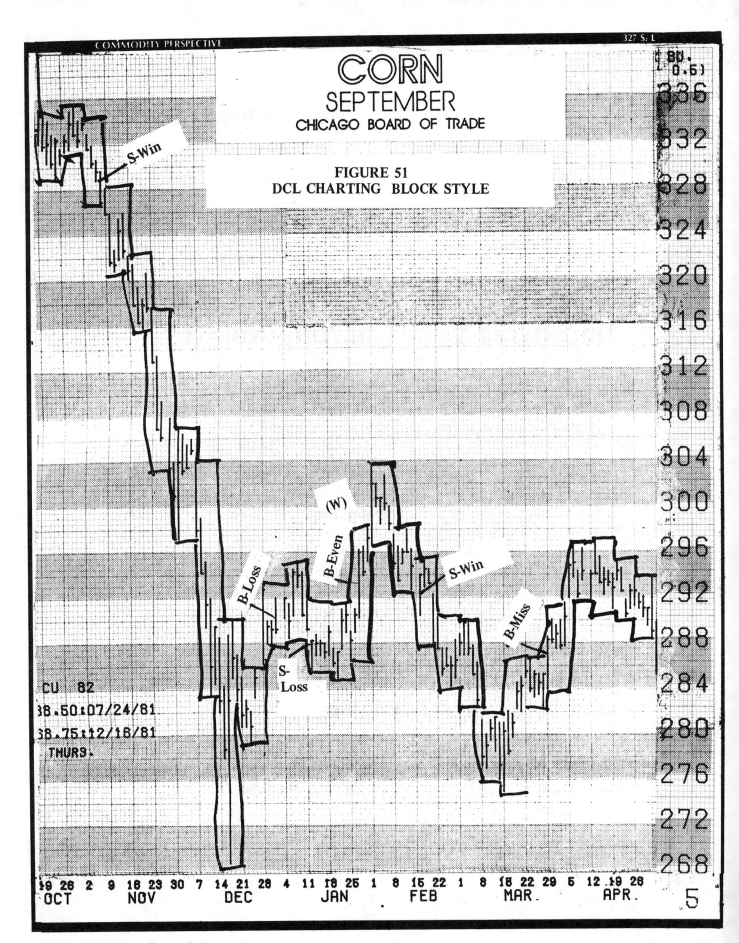

CORN
SEPTEMBER
CHICAGO BOARD OF TRADE

FIGURE 51
DCL CHARTING BLOCK STYLE

VALUE OF THE DOUBLE CHARTING TECHNIQUE

The main value is in knowing when a previous week's boundaries are exceeded. This has special significance when two or more weeks are exceeded. Breakouts are more easily seen and blocked off to show when price has moved beyond an old low or high. The current trend is more readily discerned with this charting method. You have the advantage of both weeklies and dailies on one page, with both of them visible at one time.

HOW TO USE THIS DOUBLE CHARTING TECHNIQUE

In addition to the advantages listed above, the "weekly rule" traders will find this helpful. If using the weekly rule, different commodities have various numbers of weeks that need to be surpassed before they are valid for trading. Those who use the weekly rule do a lot of testing and optimizing to find how many weeks need to be surpassed for each commodity before trading. One trader said that he used six weeks for Cotton and Wheat, and five weeks for Corn, Cattle, and Hogs. Others have given various time periods they use for the different commodities. Apparently, this changes with time and market conditions. When I learned of this method, first advocated by Donchian, it used four weeks for all commodities. With the markets becoming more volatile, many commodities now work better with two weeks, or ten trading days.

If you are using this the way it was originally taught, you must remember that it is popular and probably has a large following. Entries and exits may become hard to fill. Distortions may appear unless some changes are made. The trader needs to optimize the entries and exits every few months to know if things are changing. I'll show you how to make some changes later.

Regardless of the optimizing, if you use the original method, be prepared for large drawdowns and be capitalized to take care of them. There will be strings of losses unless you customize this method by adding your own variations.

It is important to see what is working at the present time before trading a commodity with this method, because the present pattern is apt to continue long enough for profits. What works in the recent past is most

121

likely to work when actually trading. The chances of conditions changing to fit the particular time period analyzed is expecting too much.

RULES FOR TRADING THE WEEKLY RULE METHOD

Many versions of this have been sold to the public. One trader used a variation of it for a high priced seminar. I am first going to show how it looked originally, then give a variation that greatly improves its win/loss ratio.

When you look at a page of data, you have the advantage of seeing what has already happened for the last six months, but with use in trading one does not know what will happen. To offset this, place some paper over most of the chart, so only a small part is seen. The method is simple and easy to apply, especially with our double charting technique. One strategy is to trade when the high (or low) of two weeks is passed and only get out when the high (or low) of two weeks is passed in the opposite direction. It is stop and reverse, always being in the market. These are the original rules.

When going through the trade by trade description following this explanation, I'll first give the results using the above method. Then I'll show you how to improve it for better results.

TRADING DESCRIPTIONS

Look at the example of September Corn in Figure 51. If you use two weeks, you catch the big drop rather fast, going short when price dropped below the low of the last two weeks. Then, in a more choppy market, you have two losses and a breakeven. The next two were winners. This makes six wins and two losses, or a 67% win/loss ratio. This is not bad at all.

Using the same two weeks on coffee, you can see how poorly this does (Figure 52). If it is made on close only, it does a little better. You have nine trades, with six of these losses. This is only a 33% win/loss ratio.

Some people use the weekly rule of closing beyond a certain number of weeks as an entrance method, then exit by other rules. Suppose we decide to go in on a close beyond the last two weeks price range and exit when price closes beyond the last four closes.

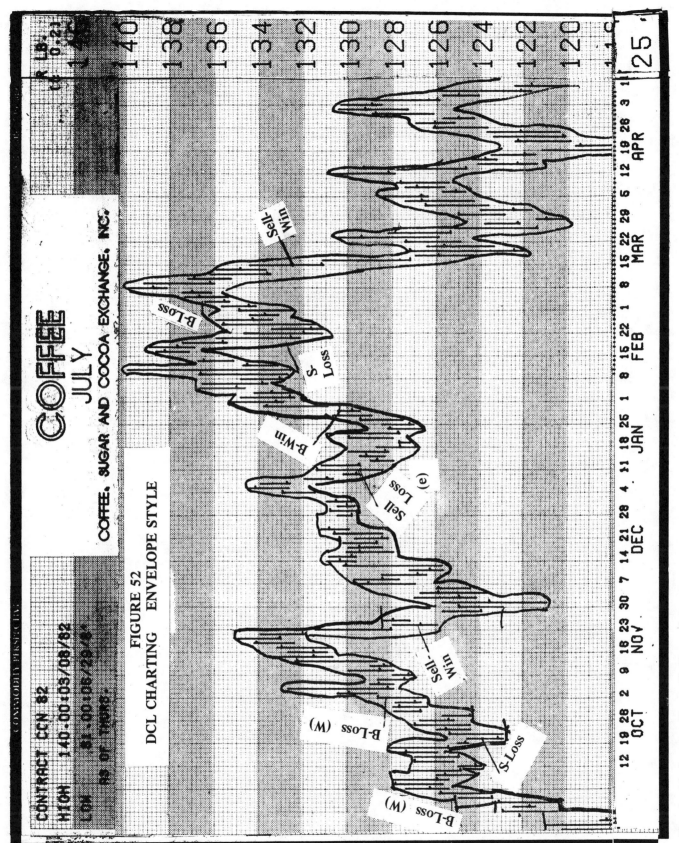

FIGURE 52
DCL CHARTING   ENVELOPE STYLE

Chart furnished courtesy Commodity Perspective

123

Back to the September Corn, you would have had seven wins and two losses with no breakeven trade. But more significant, the losses would have been much smaller.

July Coffee is also much better this way. Now you have only three losses out of nine and these losses are not as bad.

This method is ideal for optimizing. Check what number of weeks has been making the best entry method, then check what is the safest and most profitable exit rule to follow. This way you have the immediate past experience in your favor, and a much greater chance it will continue long enough to make money.

Of course, don't just optimize and expect fantastic results. Use one set system, with slight adjustments to account for changing markets.

Chapter Eight

The Quick Dominant Cycle

THE IMPORTANT THING ABOUT CYCLES

Many people spend hours each week running tests, performing complicated equations, and detrending price data trying to find the dominant cycles of a market. Most eventually go back to the simple use of dividers to pick the main recurring time spans where change should occur in the market. The important thing about cycles is finding those that are dominant.

THERE IS AN EASIER WAY

This can be done much more rapidly and accurately, as I will soon explain. You do not need to use Fourier Analysis to find a dominant cycle. All those moving averages one half the size of another can be eliminated. You still have good results, if not better, but with much less effort.

HOW IT IS DONE

First, look at price action to find repeating swings of about the same size. There are not only repeating time changes that makes cycles, but also repeating swing lengths in the market.

Take some dividers and look at a page of a chart. One soon can see that there are a number of swings of about the same size, measuring from pivot point to pivot point. In fact, on most pages of a graph, there will be several swing sizes of nearly the same dimension. These repeater swing sizes are very significant. They can be used several ways to help make money in the market. On many occasions I have found a repetitious size swing repeating as many as eight to ten times. The smaller swings will repeat more than the larger ones since there should be more of these than the larger ones.

THE SECRET OF CYCLES MADE EASY

What few people realize is that these repetitious swings are also the dominant cycle lengths of time periods in the market.

WHY THIS IS TRUE

This goes back to the theory that time and price must balance in the market. W. D. Gann called this the squaring of time and price. Price movements of equal amounts should produce time periods of nearly the same amount. If you believe the theory of balancing time and price, then you should also believe that swing sizes reveal cycle sizes. The two are based on the same principle. Check this out for yourself. I have been following this for years and know that it works.

WHAT MUST BE DONE

The price swings are on the vertical while time is represented on the charts as the horizontal lines. If you turn the price swing repeater over on the horizontal, you have the dominant cycle. Mark these at the top or bottom of the chart to see how many times they pick a new high or low. This is further proof that time and price balance and become equal. I have never known anyone to do this or associate the two in this manner. This is a new way to do some quick work in market analysis, and to get ahead of those who are less informed.

An orb, or tolerance factor, must be allowed, as is usual for those marking off repeating time spans in market turns. But it is easy to look at a price chart, pick out the swings appearing about the same size, use your dividers, and in a few minutes have solved the momentous problem so many spend so long in trying to do (see Figure 53).

USING THE DOMINANT CYCLE

Trading Rules

1. Enter a trade in the direction opposite from the direction the market has been going each time a cycle time period is reached.

2. Use the top markings for shorting; but, if the time for a change is indicated, exit and wait for a bottom mark to go long.

3. You will trade the market both long and short while in a choppy market; but in a trending market, trade only with the trend.

4. A change in trend is verified when the last two pivots have been passed. When two down pivots are passed, go short; or if two up pivots are exceeded, this is a buy signal.

5. Buy on cycles marked from bottoms and sell on cycles marked from tops.

6. Note that this exact swing size was found seven times on this chart page. When actually trading, you do not know this; so wait until three swings of about the same length are found, then start trading with these as starter cycle time periods to use until more data verifies these as being correct. In the beginning, some averaging must be done. It is usually best to use the shortest swing repeater for the beginning. This may get you out a little soon, but you can make adjustments as the future price unfolds.

TRADING APRIL LIVE CATTLE
USING THE DOMINANT CYCLE METHOD

You have found three swings of nearly the same space from peak to low by Nov. 16. Since the market has been going up, you sell at about 65.00, making sure the market is headed in your direction when starting. Cover on

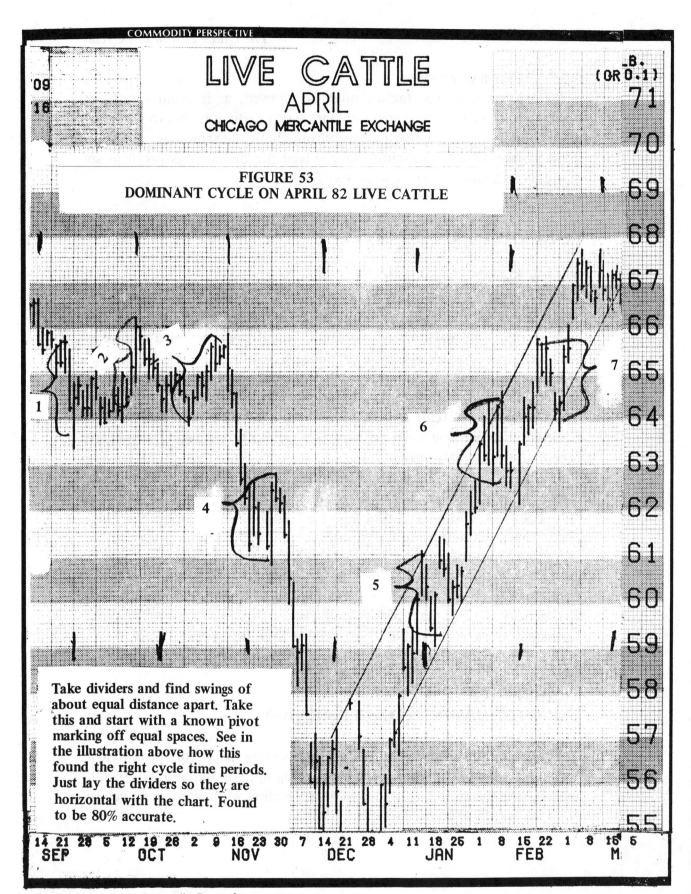

LIVE CATTLE
APRIL
CHICAGO MERCANTILE EXCHANGE

FIGURE 53
DOMINANT CYCLE ON APRIL 82 LIVE CATTLE

Take dividers and find swings of about equal distance apart. Take this and start with a known pivot marking off equal spaces. See in the illustration above how this found the right cycle time periods. Just lay the dividers so they are horizontal with the chart. Found to be 80% accurate.

Chart furnished courtesy Commodity Perspective

128

Nov. 23, when the bottom mark is reached.

You sell again when price closes decisively below the congestion on Dec. 4. Get out and stand aside when the top time period is reached (see Rule Number 2). When the bottom mark is reached, the market has been going up for three days. This is a conflict in rules, which means you still stand aside. It also indicates that a bottom is being made, because the last pivot came on a top mark and this pivot was going up when it hit a bottom mark. The reverse of the usual means a change is imminent. In this case you wait for a confirmation of a change in trend. It came on Jan. 8, when price closed above the last two pivots. This complied with the definition of a change in trend, so there is a buy signal at 57.90. Get out at 60.90, when the mark on the day of the top cycle time period is reached. Price then pulled back some. Buy on the long thrust high close day Jan. 20, on the close at 60.15. The next top cycle mark came on a down swing, so you may stay in and wait for the next top mark before getting out. With the top marks now coming so close to the same place as the bottom marks, you have reason to believe that the swing down will be short and you can stay long for a nice ride for big profits.

Those who wish may get out of this last trade on the first top mark reached after entering Jan. 20, which is on Feb. 12 at 62.90. But with the bottom mark coming up on Feb. 16, you would go long on the long range high close day of Feb. 16, and stay in until the next top dominant cycle mark on Mar. 15. The bottom mark would put you back long on the 17th of March, but we are too near the end of data to count this as a trade.

It is necessary to say that meats, grains, and other farm products follow cycles better than some other commodities. But if you will use these rules and instructions, you will find many more chances to use the quick cycle method to make a lot of money.

Chapter Nine

Using Activity Indicators

INTRODUCTION

For the sophisticated trader, a chart shows much more than just price activity. It also shows range activity, momentum or changes in velocity, the amount of volume on or before a reversal day, and lets the trader compare these with known leaders of a complex. You do not need a lot of oscillators to tell you these things. Your eyes should be trained to take these things in with a visual examination of the chart.

WHAT SOME TRADERS HAVE DONE

There are many combinations of oscillators that help identify market activity. Some combine volume with price, others use the daily range with price momentum. You have, without a doubt, seen charts with wavy lines, diagonal lines, and various lines running this way and that over the page. All this does not necessarily mean that more is being accomplished, however. There are certain things that are important and which can be checked off each day when doing analysis. There are easy, quick ways to do this.

WHAT IS IMPORTANT?

It is necessary to keep your analysis simple. Too much to do does not leave time for reflecting and summarizing one's thoughts. The activity of the chart needs to be noted for the various changes and set down so it can be easily assimilated into meaningful conclusions.

It is important to make comparisons within the complex, and between the various indicators. There are a number of questions that ought to be answered each day. How is volume doing on this long range day? Is this also true with the leader of the complex? I will give a more complete list of important questions later, in the activity indicator list. But for now think about ways to check these quickly without a lot of work. This can be done!

Why spend a lot of time averaging the daily range of the last ten, twenty, or forty days? You can look at a chart, use your dividers, and get a good approximation of the average daily range. Outside days with a long range can be quickly noted, and are significant. If the price is moving up faster, the angle will be steeper and larger. Comparison of leaders and various options can be done by laying several days of price pages down beside each other. Find the activity facts that you think are important and make a list of these to make sure nothing is missed as you go over them each day.

Before making a complete list, think about the values of various indicators. Some will help more than others. One that many analysts overlook is the long range day. See Figure 54, where there are long range days occurring close to five of the six main pivots. This is one of the best indicators to watch, and is the easiest, most simple of them all. Sometimes the long range day comes near the end of a move. If it is after an extended move of the market, suspect an exhaust. Take this as a warning signal. But keep a close look for outside days or long range days, as they usually go with a change of trend.

Another activity indicator easily followed but often overlooked is the breadth of a market. In other words, how long has the trading base been building? The length of time involved in accumulation and distribution is important to know. The longer it takes for a base to be built or a top to be made, the more important this is. So do not overlook these important things when making the activity list.

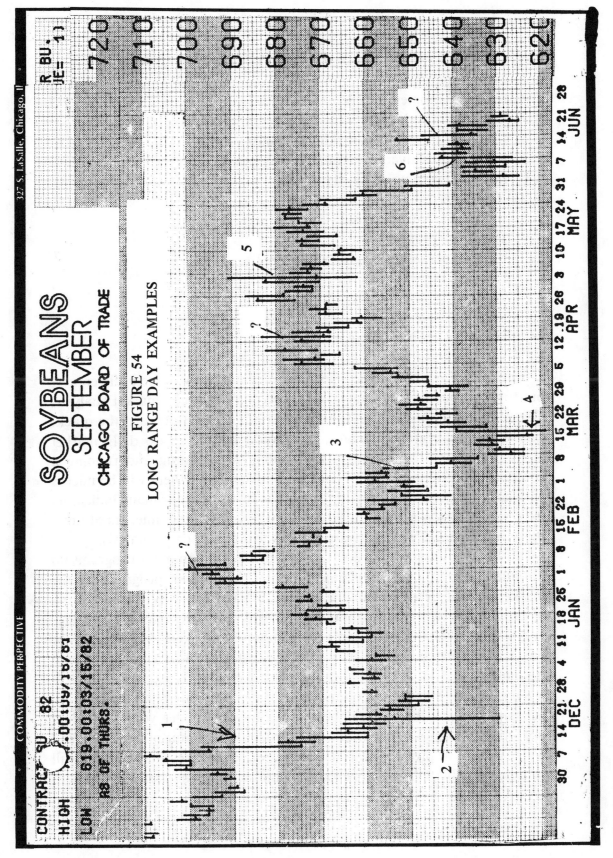

FIGURE 54
LONG RANGE DAY EXAMPLES

SOYBEANS
SEPTEMBER
CHICAGO BOARD OF TRADE

133

SUGGESTED LIST OF VARIOUS ACTIVITY INDICATORS
1. Long range day?
2. Increased momentum?
3. Length of base?
4. Leader of the complex making a change?
5. Back months diverging from front months?
6. Increased volume on key day?
7. New highs or new lows?
8. Wall lines coming across?
9. Trend line broken ?
10. Multipivot line converging with price?

IS A COMPUTER NECESSARY?

The kind of operation the trader has will naturally make a difference, but for most people a computer is not necessary for daily market analysis. The computer is needed for testing and optimizing. But learn the quick, simple methods, as I've taught, and you'll be abe to do daily market analysis quicker than going to the trouble of updating and running a computer program on a microcomputer. Eventually, there will be micros with larger in-core memory and storage capacity, whereby many indicators may be tested over a lot of different contracts in a short time. As of now, this is not available with software that is adequate for daily analysis.

It is best for the trader to do his own work. Most computer programs do not allow altering or customizing. Many of the analysis programs on the market do not even explain the theory and reasons why the indicators offered should work. You should know why you are winning or losing, and this requires analytical tools understood by a trader. My advice is to buy trading programs you may alter or customize to fit your personal trading.

Those who manage accounts must have computers to be able to accomplish what they should be doing. But do not let your individual operation be compared with that of a broker or account manager. If you will take time to properly learn the indjcators of market analysis, you will be able to do better than an account manager, since the manager needs to

134

work with large groups of people to pay for his much bigger overhead. Most of the vital market indicators are simple and easy to use.

SUGGESTED ACTIVITY INDEX

1. Long Range Day	30%
2. Increased Momentum	10%
3. Leader Comparisons	15%
4. Back Month, Front Month Divergences	20%
5. Increased Key-Day Volume	15%
6. New Highs or New Lows	10%
	100%

This gives suggested values to place on the various activity indicators. It would not take much work (with a calculator) to use the checklist, then add up the values as they are found. Your "yes" or "no" check marks then become part of a composite answer for the activity of each day.

The Index is valuable as a warning signal to keep you out of trouble and to help preserve gains. But, please also use other indicators when trading.

THE VALUE OF THE LONG RANGE DAY

Years ago an old pro told me to watch for outside days in the market. He said these were tipoffs that a change was about to take place. For a long time I was involved in more complicated analyses. Now that I have come back to test this simple indicator, I wish I'd done it sooner.

TRADING WITH THE
LONG RANGE DAY INDICATOR

It seems too simple to be true, but you'll be amazed at the results shown at the end of this chapter. But first, here is how it is done.

Look at the September 82 Soybean chart. On December 1 there was a long range day, of about twice the length of the range for the previous ten days. Four days later there was a change of direction. Then on December 8 there was another long range day, even longer than any other previous long range day. This was confirmation that the market was going down. But on December 16 there was a long range day larger than that of December 8. It took six days before there was a change of directions; but when it came, it lasted for six weeks!

On January 27 there was a long range day, and on February 2 there was another one of about the same size. After this, there was a six week drop in the market.

There were smaller long range days on the rally starting February 23 and ending March 3, but the signficant long range day came on March 15. This was also a double bottom and proved to be a tip off for a four week rally.

The reaction around mid-April was forecasted by a long range day on April 13.

The real test of a change in trend came on April 30, when there was an exceedingly large long range day. Price immediately went down, then struggled back up for about two weeks. But it could not go far. The uphill fight was over on May 24.

There can be two long range days fairly close that give different answers. See the last two weeks of data, on the bottom right side of the September Soybean chart. On June 8 there was a long range day signaling an uptrend, but five trading days later there was another long range day indicating another turn of the market. In a case like this, you must go with the major trend, which was still down.

SUMMARY OF LONG RANGE TESTING INFORMATION

1. The close does not have to be in the direction of the change. Just the fact a long range day occurs is significant.
2. There can be at least five days before the change comes.
3. The long range day does not indicate how much of a change to expect.
4. Always look for a change in the opposite direction—unless a change has already taken place in the last two days.
5. If a change has just occurred, count the long range day as

confirmation of a change.

With this information, testing was done to develop trading rules based upon the long range day. Here, again, I am using one indicator only to be able to test it. You would use it in conjunction with others when actually trading.

TRADING RULES FOR LONG RANGE DAYS

1. Use the last ten days of data for range comparisons. Look for days that are about twice the average size.

2. Compare a long range day with others that previously came on turning points, or near turning points of the market.

3. Wait for a close beyond the last two closes in the direction of the trade. Use this to enter the market after a long range day. It must be in the opposite direction from the way the market was traveling during the last five days. Do not use this in congestions.

4. Do not exit until another long range day gives a signal.

5. Re-enter the market, if no change of trend has occurred, when there is a close beyond the last four closes. This is assuming the last change was a small pullback, and that the trend is apparently continuing.

RESULTS OF TRADING LONG RANGE DAYS

1. Sold on December 8, out on December 16. (These trades are on the close). Made 21¢. Bought on December 23 at 659. Out on January 19 at 666. Made 7¢. Bought again on January 26. Out on February 2 for 21¢ profit. Sold on February 3, out on February 26, making 5¢. Bought on March 15 at 639 and covered on April 13 at 669, making 30¢. Bought again on April 21 at 669, out on April 30 at 671, making 2¢. Sold on May 5 and covered on the next long range day of June 7 at 642, making 29¢. Bought on June 7 at 642. Covered on June 14 at 635, losing 16¢.

These are seven trades with one loss. Moneywise, you would have had 115¢ made at $50.00 a cent, or $5,750.00. You lost 16¢ at $50.00 a cent for $800.00. Assuming $100.00 per trade for commission, this is a net gain of $4,250.00.

Chapter Ten

The DMA Trading Method

I. WHAT THIS DOES

DMA means Discretionary Moving Average. As the name states, some moving averages are part of this method, but they are used in a special discretionary way. The Moving Averages are part of the theory, but being discretionary in picking the methods for the various kinds of markets is more important. Each market has its own strategy in DMA trading.

II. KINDS OF MARKETS

We divide the market price patterns into four categories (see Figure 55). These are: The congestion, the labored move, the swinging market, and the runaway.

    1. The congestion is defined as any market that has short up and down price movements, with the highs in the same general price range and the lows also in their own price vicinity. The congestion may be on a slight slant or angle as well as straight across. For our purposes here, we trade the congestion the same as we do the labored move.

    2. The labored move is similar to the congestion, except it has a

FIGURE 55
TYPES OF MARKETS

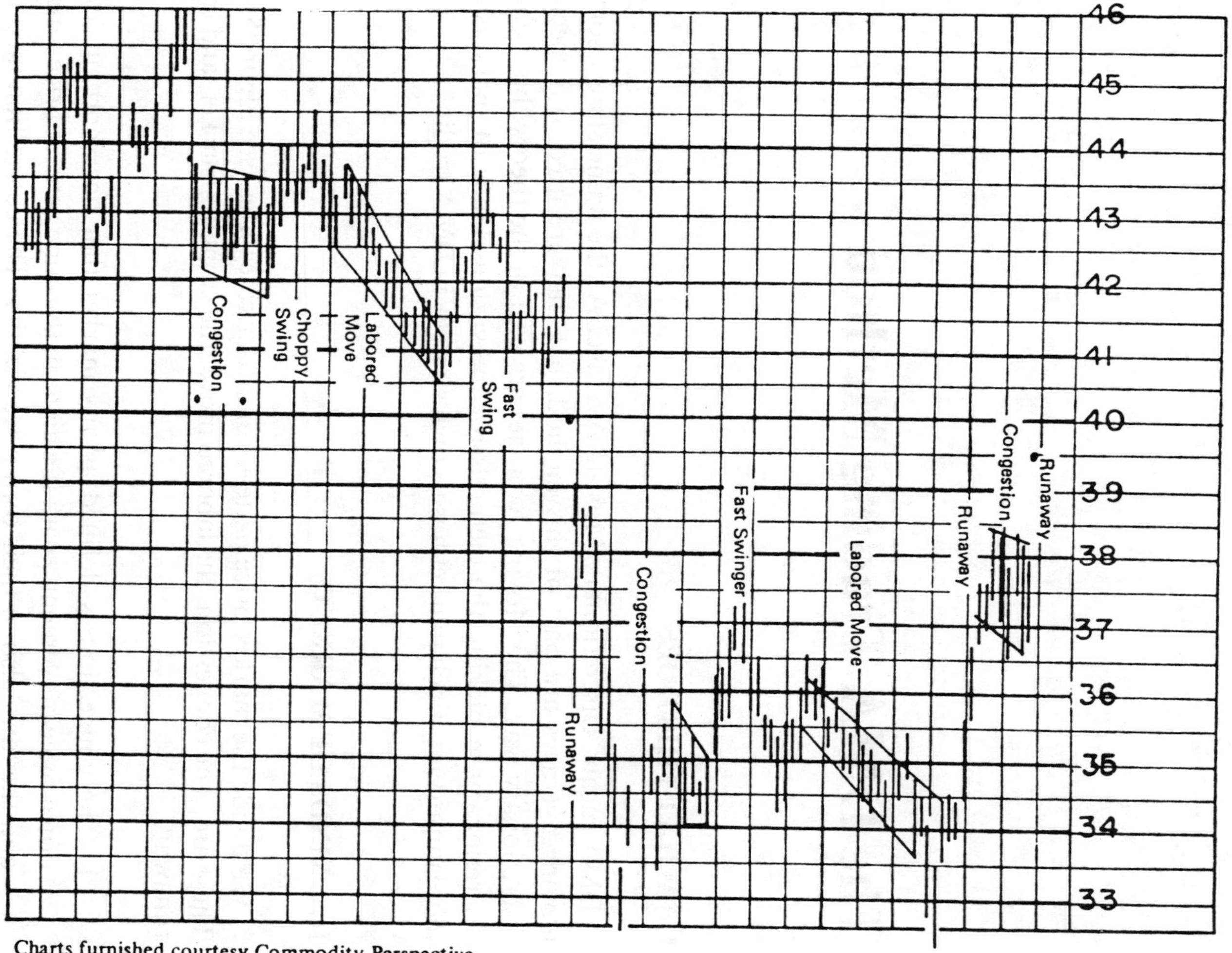

Charts furnished courtesy Commodity Perspective

140

definite slope and moves in a channel price action.

3. Swinging markets move up and down in a choppy or zig-zag manner. There may be fast swingers that go up and down rapidly, or slow choppy ones.

4. Runaway markets are like swingers, except they always go up fast and continue further than the fast swingers.

5. The difference between the labored move and the congestion:

    a. The congestion has a more flat, or sideways, movement.

    b. The labored move must be more than four swings that stop within a definite boundary or channel. It also is slanted at least 30 degrees or more (a definite slope).

    c. The labored move should go further than the congestion. Most congestions will have no more than six swings.

    d. Some congestions will develop into labored moves. It is also possible for a labored move to swing back and make an irregular congestion. You always follow the last two pivot lines until a pattern is definite.

6. The difference between swinging and runaway markets:

    a. A fast five days run, then a congestion, denotes a runaway type market.

    b. When the angle of travel is almost straight up (or down) for five days, consider this a runaway and not a swinger.

    c. If a market has been traveling a long way for a period of two or more months, then reverses and makes a gap, consider this a breakaway gap and the beginning of a runaway. A second gap coming close to the first gives further confirmation that this is a runaway and should move a good distance.

III. THE SOUND THEORY OF THE DMA

This method is based on a very sound theory that has been tested by computer. Of course, I cannot guarantee anyone will make money, but I do feel that you should. This technique covers all obstacles involved in beating the market. It is a trending method that usually also makes good in non-trending markets.

J. M. Keynes, in an article published in *80 Micro magazine*, used three moving averages and guaranteed that it would make money even though only four out of ten trades were good. The DMA method uses some of the same theory, but includes techniques that produce a better trading record (according to testing).

IV.   HOW TO MAKE MONEY WITH THIS METHOD

The only way to succeed in any business is to be in control of what you are doing, then only do business in the manner necessary to make money. Relating this to the commodity trading business requires developing the right strategy for each kind of market, then trading these markets properly.

It really amazes me that so many people use the same trading method on all kinds of markets. Some traders have a non-trending system to go with a trending, but this is not enough. The DMA is a method that considers all kinds of markets and trades each of them differently.

It is also important to understand that a lot of market price action is random in nature, so you must devise a way to discount this random action or to get around price motions that cause losses. A trading plan is not good unless it has a built-in method avoiding the random movement of the markets. In the DMA, this is done for you.

Another factor in success is starting at the right time. Farmers do not try to plow in the rainy season and neither should a trader try to trade in a market that is not following the usual rules of orderliness. If you cannot decide what kind of market you are in, you should stand aside until you are sure of how to trade properly. There is a right time and a wrong time to begin. Use some of the cycle techniques presented in earlier chapters to help get off to a better start.

Diversification is also important. This means using at least five different kinds of commodities. Find types that do not follow each other. Some, like lumber and interest rates, move together most of the time. Pick a grain, a meat, a metal, an interest rate, and perhaps a food. Try to stay in the markets that are moving, rather than the choppy ones (see Figure 56 for examples of non-orderly markets).

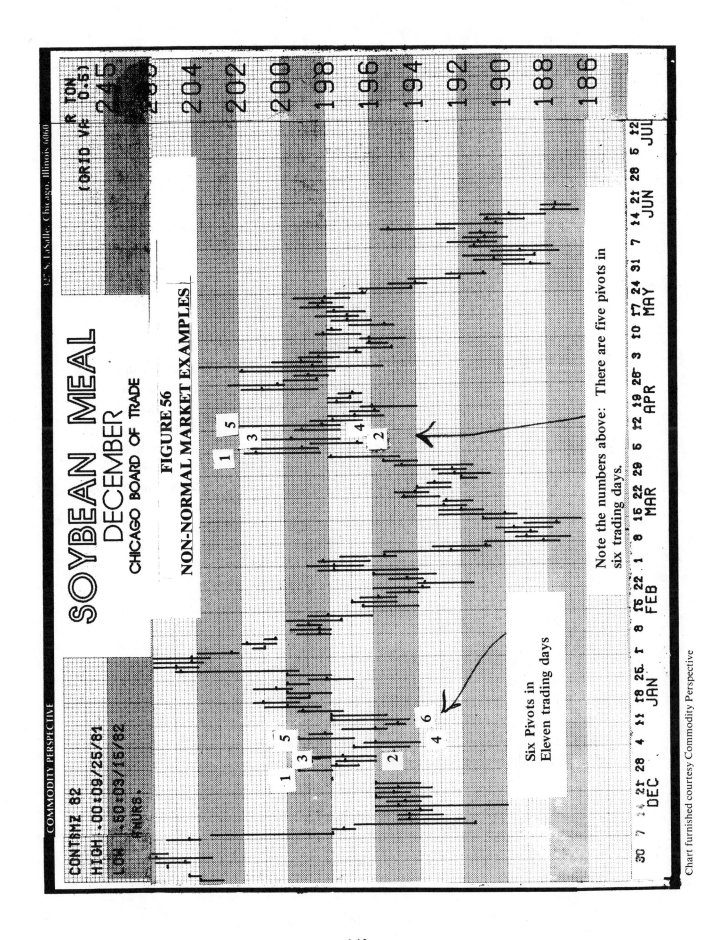

FIGURE 56
NON-NORMAL MARKET EXAMPLES

SOYBEAN MEAL
DECEMBER
CHICAGO BOARD OF TRADE

Note the numbers above: There are five pivots in six trading days.

Six Pivots in Eleven trading days

Chart furnished courtesy Commodity Perspective

143

To Summarize:

- Trade differently for each kind of market.
- Trade only in orderly markets that are moving.
- Have a good filtering method to take out the random movement.
- Get started when a cycle is with you.
- Keep at it, even though there may be several losses in a row. Consistency and persistency will pay off.

V. HOW TO FILTER OUT RANDOM MOVEMENT

Proper use of moving averages will filter out a lot of random movement in the market. This is one part of the method. Next, use a directional indicator, and only trade in the direction it indicates. This will filter out a great deal of the larger random movement of the market. This usually eliminates most of the abnormal swings of the market. By abnormal, I mean sudden moves caused by strike scares, government intervention, weather scares, etc. If there is some merit to one of these scares, it will be indicated by the directional indicator giving a signal. Until it does, stay out and be a winner.

Channeling is another method of filtering out undesired price moves. So you can use moving averages, channeling, and directional indicators all to filter out movements you shouldn't trade.

VI. WORK REQUIRED

Keep charts to trade the DMA, as the type of market is important. When appropriate, draw channel lines. There is a computer program that will do a lot of this, but charts must still be kept to pick the kind of market being traded. It does not take much experience to be able to distinguish one market pattern from another, and it is necessary for trading the DMA. To update five commodities and run the computer programs will not take much time.

VII. REQUIREMENTS FOR TRADING

To trade the DMA, anyone should have available about $25,000.00 in speculative money. Anything less would require trading only the slow moving, lower priced commodities. It is best to be diversified with the DMA. If you can't find at least five different commodities in different complexes of the market, then go to the mini-contracts, such as those on the Mid-Am Exchange.

VIII. USING MOVING AVERAGES

You will be using moving averages to help filter out some of the random movements of the market. One of the oldest and most often used is the four, nine, and eighteen day method. Doubtless many people have found ways to use this for making money, or it would not have been used so often and so long. If you find that too many traders are using these, causing bad fills, you can optimize by adding or subtracting a number from each of these three, making either three or five, seven or ten, and seventeen or nineteen. The exact number of days does not make much difference, but may help you get ahead of other traders.

Do not use these moving averages the way most people do, however. If your other rules agree, buy or sell when the four crosses the nine, but only use the longer term moving average for a directional indicator when trading the swinging, zigzag, and runaway type of markets. The congestion and labored move require no directional indicators unless they have been part of a runaway. If the market goes out of a runaway into a congestion or labored move, you should use the directional indicator. Choppy areas that have congestion and labored moves do not need a directional indicator, so do not use the long term moving average here. The long term moving average is used to filter out larger types of random movement in the market; but if the market is choppy, there is no larger movement to filter.

IX. GENERAL RULES

If the trader is using a computer program, it should have its methods optimized and ready to use. For those who want to do their own testing and work out their own program, we advise the following rules:

1. Run the variations of the moving averages to see what is working best at that time.

2. A channel is started when three pivots have been made, with no more than four trading days in the swing of each pivot. This gives you the ability to draw the 0-2 lines across, tip-to-tip, on the two pivots; and a parallel to this through the opposite-side pivot between those two. This makes the 0-2 channel. Go from one 0-2 configuration to another, making lines each time two new pivots are formed, always using the last two pivots for the channel line (see Figure 57).

3. Consider everything with an angle of 30 degrees or less (where the 0-2 lines are concerned) to be either a congestion or a labored move. Make an exception to this when the congestions or labored moves emerge out of the fast swinging or runaway markets.

4. Stand aside anytime there is a tight one or two day up and down movement. These usually do not give enough room for making profits.

Also do not trade wildly gyrating markets. (See the illustration of non-normal markets, Figure 56).

5. Use the section of this book on trading cycles to help pick the best time to begin trading.

X. SPECIFIC TRADING RULES

1. *Labored Move or Congestion*

   a. The labored move must have three swings of more than two days each swing, but not more than four in each, before a trade is initiated. The congestion is traded the same way. You never know when a congestion will turn into a labored move, or vice versa.

   b. To buy, there must be a high close day in the lower part of the channel. To sell, there must be a low close day in the upper part of the channel. You always buy in the lower 25% of the range of the channel or sell in the upper 25% (see Figure 58).

   c. Exit a long trade when the lower channel line is crossed. On a sell signal, exit when the upper channel line is crossed.

   d. If you are in the market when a labored move begins, switch to these rules for trading. If there has been a runaway or fast swinging market before one of these, you must only trade with the

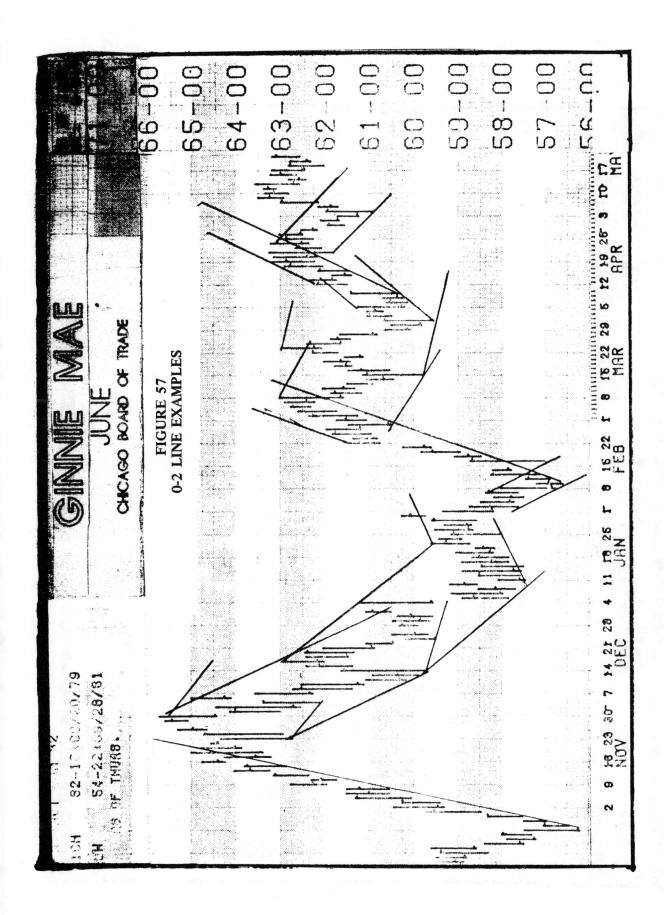

GINNIE MAE
JUNE
CHICAGO BOARD OF TRADE

FIGURE 57
0-2 LINE EXAMPLES

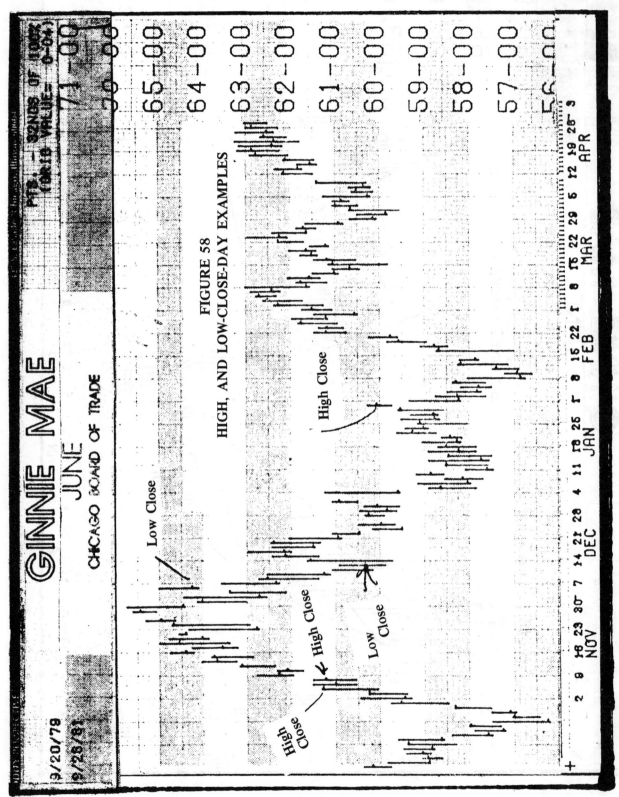

FIGURE 58

HIGH, AND LOW-CLOSE-DAY EXAMPLES

Chart furnished courtesy Commodity Perspective

148

directional indicator. A good directional indicator is the eighteen day DMA.

2. *Swinging Market*

a. You must have the long term moving average pointed in the direction you are to trade, unless the lows and highs are in about the same price zone, with the swings making a sideways movement.

b. To confirm that it's a swinging market, rather than a labored move or congestion, the breakout must be 15% more than the range of the channel, and you must have a close beyond the center of the day (in the direction of the trade). The close must be above (or below) the channel line.

c. Enter the swinging trade when the four day moving average crosses the nine in the direction you wish to trade, according to your directional indicator.

d. A stop loss of about $500.00 should be entered above or below the trade when entering.

e. Exit the trade when price closes below (or above, if short) the last two previous closes.

f. Re-enter, if there has been no change of trend, when the last four closes are passed.

3. *Runaway Market*

a. The long term moving average must be pointed in the direction of the trade.

b. Exit the runaway when the close is beyond the previous four closes.

c. When entering, put in a stop loss where desired, usually of about $500.00.

d. An alternate exit can be used by exiting the trade when the four day moving average crosses the nine (in a direction away from the trade).

e. Re-enter, if there has been no change of trend, when the last four closes are passed.

IN CONCLUSION

If you want to optimize or vary this system, do some of the following:

1. Change the moving averages.
2. Make the entry or exit signals easier or harder by changing the number of days the close may be beyond previous closes.
3. Change the percent amount required for a confirmation of a break from a congestion or labored move.

This is not a glamorous top or bottom picking method, but it is a safe, conservative method that makes money. It satisfies even the most skeptical traders, as long as they agree that once a market starts going in a direction, it tends to keep going. The DMA waits to confirm which way the market is going, it filters out random movement, and stays out of most bad trades. It is a good workhorse of a system that should consistently make money each year for those who will patiently use it.

Chapter Eleven

Fast Or Slow Trading

INTRODUCTION

When trying to position yourself in the market, many questions come up. The trader must decide if the entrance signal is strong or weak. Will there be a pullback? What is the profit potential? Should this be a short term or a long term trade? How fast should one act? These questions need to be answered. Profits, and maybe losses, depend on the answers.

Sadly, many traders rely on hearsay, then must learn the hard way—in the market. Testing and optimizing is needed to learn what to expect. Paper trading and experience are the only ways to become a good trader.

There are too many variations to a lot of rules, so the only thing that makes a winner is doing your own work. This research will help, but every trader must develop his own style and method. Most of these questions can be answered by understanding congestion patterns, price reversal patterns, characteristics of a commodity, and pullback distance relationships. These all take on different meanings at different levels of a commodity's progress. Usually, the economic conditions affecting supply and demand do not change fast. What has been happening in the past usually keeps happening long enough to make a profit.

151

I. WHAT MUST BE DONE

The first step is knowing the current stage of the market. A reversal price pattern to go long does not mean much in a rapidly falling bear market. This is oversimplified to bring out my point, but is more important when applied to complex situations.

It's also important to know the characteristics of commodities—how they react at different levels and in various kinds of markets.

The last step is to apply this information according to the momentum or steepness of travel. Various commodities behave differently according to various degrees of momentum at various levels of price action.

The first example is June 83 Live Hogs (see Figure 59). For seven months it was rather choppy, but gradually went higher. The bottoms and tops were mostly "V" shaped or inverted "V's." There were many congestions and labored moves. Three repetitious swings can be found, if you check closely. Realizing this is the beginning is very helpful, since the same type of thing continued for six months. Now I'll get a little more specific and also go into more complex and exciting implications.

II. WHAT CONGESTIONS WILL TELL

To understand congestions, you must consider their size and shape, the way the market breaks out of each, and the length of time they consume. The distance between the congestions is also important.

The first thing to realize about congestions is that the longer price stays in a congestion, the more important it is. The breakout from a three month triangle or congestion is much more potent than one of only three weeks.

You must also observe the closeness of the last congestions. Congestions coming close together imply a choppy market, which should continue until the congestions get further apart. What has been happening is likely to keep happening. See the June 83 Hog Chart (Fig. 59) for an example of this. There should not be large congestions following each other. Large congestions should be followed by smaller ones. The significance of distances between congestions will be discussed more later.

How "tall" the congestion is also gives vital information. Tall congestions with more than two days of movement in one direction mean something totally different from the short or more narrow type.

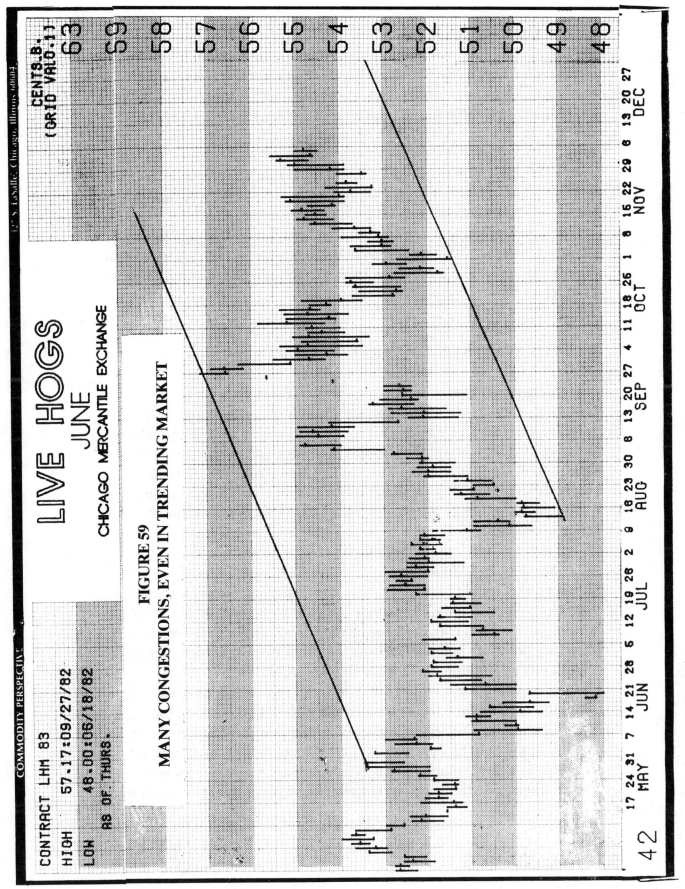

LIVE HOGS
JUNE
CHICAGO MERCANTILE EXCHANGE

FIGURE 59
MANY CONGESTIONS, EVEN IN TRENDING MARKET

153

You should normally find the tall type of congestions near the top of a move. Swings coming further apart show that there is more demand when in an up market; those shorter and closer together have more supply. This relation to the last stage of a market for tall congestions must be considered according to the usual characteristics of a commodity. Some commodities are thin in volume and open interest, which causes them to have more tall congestions, since they swing around a lot more than others that have a better following.

When there are variances from the usual, this should alert the trader that change is in order. Tall congestions in bottoming action usually mean that the market is about to move away from the bottom. See the Dec. 81 Swiss Franc chart for an example of this (Figure 60).

III. THE STAGES OF A MARKET

1. *Beginning Types*
Markets coming off of bottoms should not normally travel at a steep angle or with fast acceleration. When the market gets near historical lows (adjusted for inflation), then trends sideways for several months, be suspicious of sharp breakouts. This could be the erratic run up or down of accumulation. Normally, markets move off of the bottom on about a forty-five degree angle, or less. Expect quick pullbacks when there is fast action during bottoms.

2. *Second Level Markets*
This market should proceed near or above a forty-five degree angle. If there has been good bottoming action followed by a good leg up off of the bottom, then a good congestion or choppy area, next one should expect a faster, steeper climb in the second level. A break below the forty-five angle is much more significant here than in the first leg action.

Many people do not realize that, just as there are double and triple bottom or tops, likewise there may be double and triple swings in the stages of a market. The first leg up may have three swings of about the same length. See the Feb. 83 Pork Bellies chart, Figure 61, for an illustration of three legs in a down market. These three legs are really one move of the market. Generally, the same pattern repeats no more than two times in a

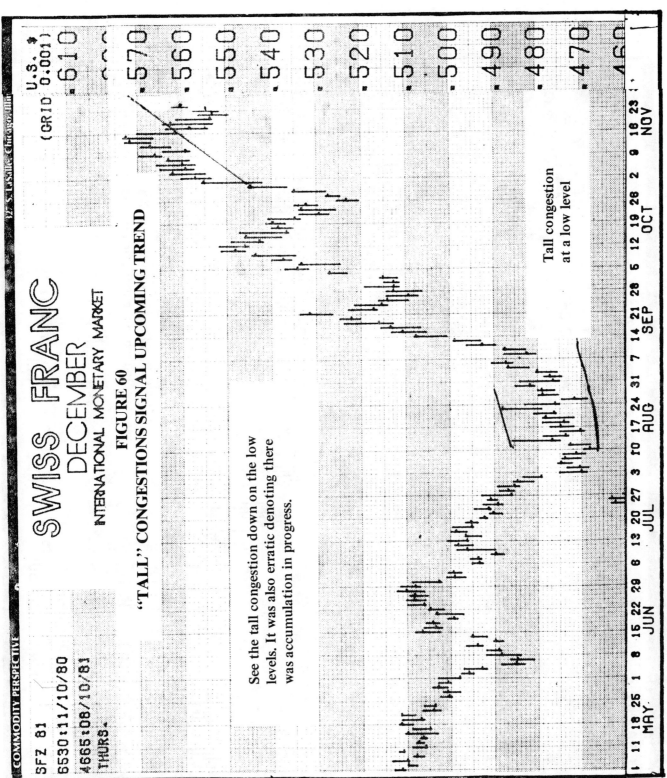

COMMODITY PERSPECTIVE

SFZ 81   U.S. $
6530:11/10/80   (GRID 0.001)   .610
4665:08/10/81
THURS.

SWISS FRANC
DECEMBER
INTERNATIONAL MONETARY MARKET
FIGURE 60

'TALL' CONGESTIONS SIGNAL UPCOMING TREND

See the tall congestion down on the low
levels. It was also erratic denoting there
was accumulation in progress.

Tall congestion
at a low level

Chart furnished courtesy Commodity Perspective

155

FIGURE 61
THREE LEGS IN A MARKET TREND

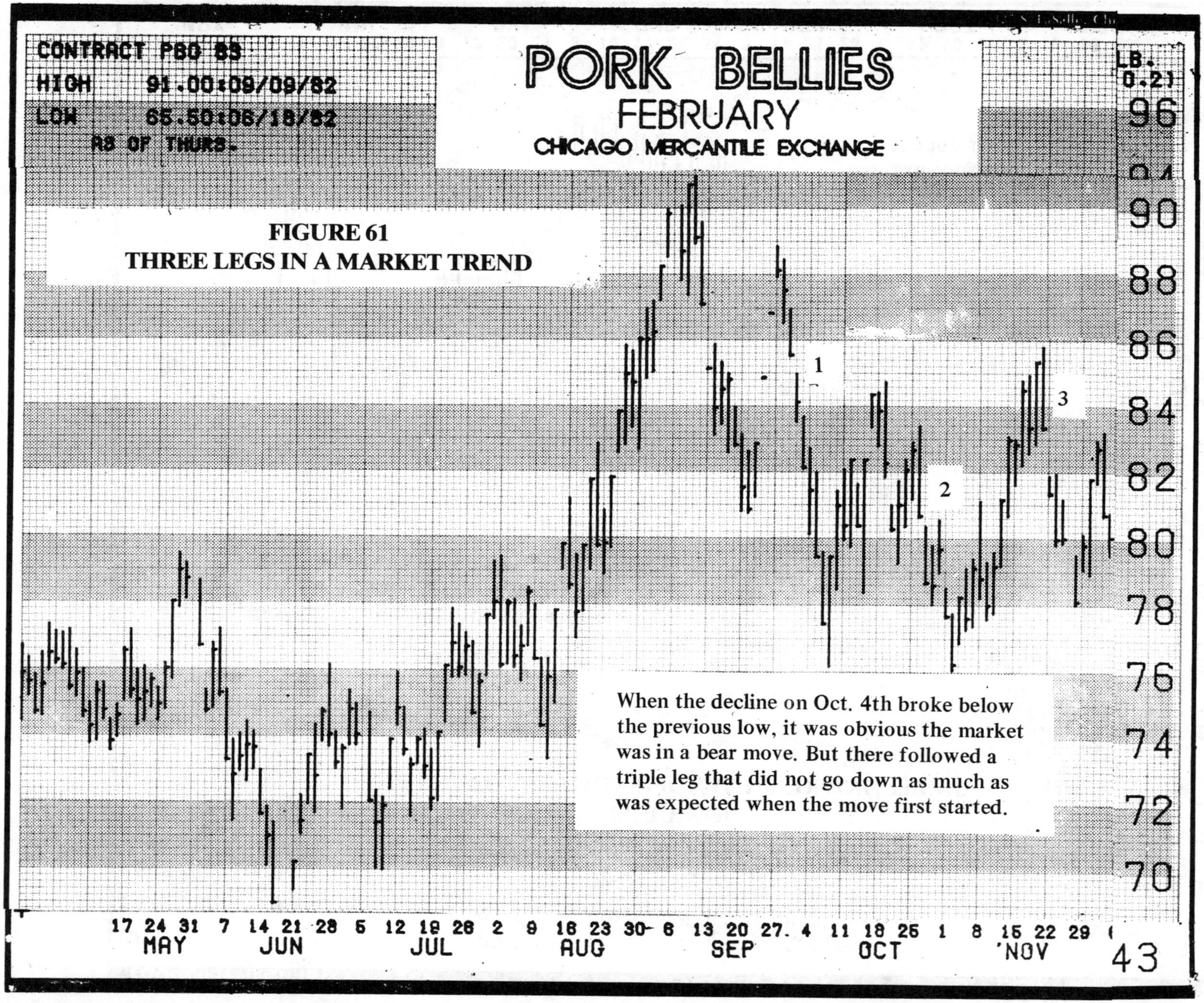
CONTRACT PBO 83
HIGH 91.00:09/09/82
LOW 65.50:06/18/82
AS OF THURS.
PORK BELLIES
FEBRUARY
CHICAGO MERCANTILE EXCHANGE
LB.
0.2)
96
90
88
86
84
82
80
78
76
74
72
70
1
2
3
When the decline on Oct. 4th broke below the previous low, it was obvious the market was in a bear move. But there followed a triple leg that did not go down as much as was expected when the move first started.
17 24 31 7 14 21 28 5 12 19 26 2 9 16 23 30 6 13 20 27 4 11 18 25 1 8 15 22 29
MAY JUN JUL AUG SEP OCT NOV
43

Chart furnished courtesy Commodity Perspective

row. When there have been two stages of about the same kind of price action, then expect the next to be different.

Going from bottom to top, the last level is usually faster and steeper than the others and also has fewer congestions.

Triangles and swinging sideways movements are more common at the end of the second level. This is the fourth leg pullback from the third leg of the Elliott count.

3. *The Third Level Market*

Sharp, fast action is expected here. Extensions or elongated legs are more common. Larger reactions than usual should be viewed as topping action. If there has been sharper than normal first and second level market action, the third level may be only a big swinging affair, with several large up and down legs in it.

Everything is dependent on what has happened before. All market action tells its tale to those who know how to read it. The size, shape and time involved for all swings is important. The rules for squaring time and price come to play. If a market goes up too fast, expect sideways action until the time and price periods are about the same. On the other hand, if the market has failed to achieve the level of price that the time period indicates it should, then expect fast action to let price catch up with time.

IV. WHAT REACTIONS AND RALLIES REVEAL

A reaction is a pullback in a bull market and a rally is a pullback in a bear market. The most important thing to consider about rallies or reactions is: "What level or stage is the market in?"

1. *Factors That Denote Strength*
See the 83 Plywood chart, Figure 62.

The smaller the pullback, the stronger the move. If the market is making big swings or rolls instead of one good leg, then a pullback may be only a congestion period in these swings. There is not much meaning to a pullback in a market that is not going anywhere.

157

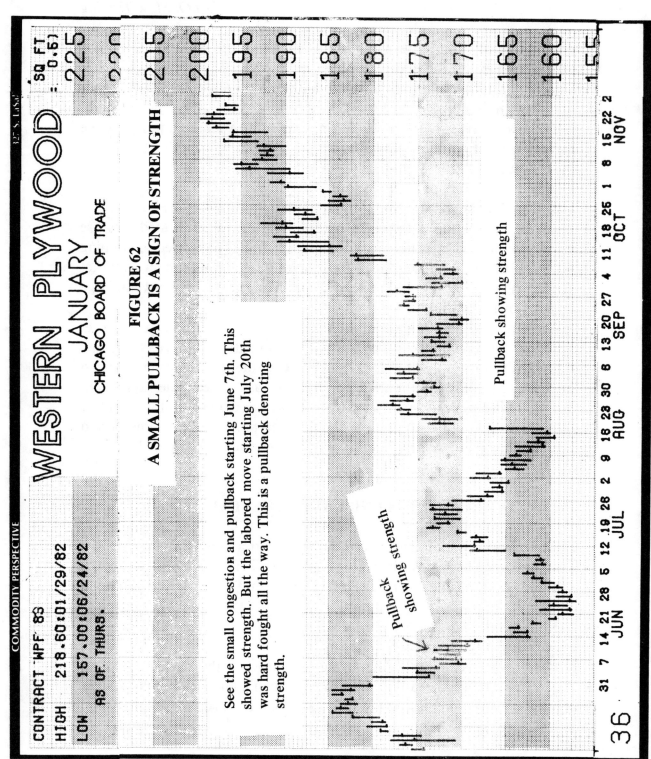

COMMODITY PERSPECTIVE

CONTRACT WPF 83
HIGH 218.60:01/29/82
LOW 157.00:06/24/82
AS OF THURS.

WESTERN PLYWOOD
JANUARY
CHICAGO BOARD OF TRADE

SQ FT
= 0.6)

FIGURE 62
A SMALL PULLBACK IS A SIGN OF STRENGTH

See the small congestion and pullback starting June 7th. This showed strength. But the labored move starting July 20th was hard fought all the way. This is a pullback denoting strength.

Pullback showing strength

Pullback showing strength

158

2. *Factors That Denote Weakness*

The larger the pullback in a market movement, the weaker it is considered to be. But what may be considered a normal-sized movement is what is important. The trader must note how far a market goes in a period of time. If the time period of the pullback is much longer than usual, even though it may not be any greater in height, this implies weakness of a move. This is especially true if the move is already square with price and the time amount is now running into that of the next leg of the market.

V. CHARACTERISTICS OF A COMMODITY MARKET

1. *Erratic Market*

See Dec. 81 Swiss Franc chart in Figure 60.

Some markets are by nature more erratic. These usually are the thinner commodities, without much following. Markets like cocoa and coffee that are influenced by foreign governments are usually more erratic also, especially when they're falling. One never knows when the government may decide to support these commodities. Foreign currencies are the same. They may have a good pullback going, then suffer a complete collapse as the government stops its support.

2. Cyclic Market

Some commodities follow seasonals and cycles better than others. Meats and grains fall into this category. Those more subject to regular rhythm in the market are the perishables like eggs, potatoes, and pork bellies. But while these follow a good cyclic pattern, they are usually more erratic on a short term basis because they are often dominated by large speculators. Traders need to be well-financed to trade these markets.

Commodities following the longer cycles based on the economy of the country are copper, cotton, and lumber.

3. *The GT's*

GT stands for government tampering. We have already mentioned the Currencies, but along with them are the Interest Rate and Stock Index futures.

The ease or restriction of credit usually makes the Stock Indexes move, as well as Gold and Silver. Lumber seldom trends against the T-Bill futures. If you are to trade these GT Markets, you should learn what indicators are used by the Federal Open Market Committee, then do your analysis work on these statistics, just as you do on that of the futures.

Occasionally a commodity will become a government football, such as Wheat during the Carter Administration. A lot of small traders were wiped out on that grain embargo.

One must take the newspapers seriously when they mention strikes and embargoes. This is also true with tariffs or restrictions on imports. But more important is the fact that the market usually lets you know in advance when this sort of thing is underfoot. It is shown by erratic movements in what has formerly been an orderly market. This erratic movement means that insiders, who know more about what is going on with government bureaus, have leaked the news to their friends and kin.

Anyone trading GT markets needs to keep his ear close to the ground and run scared when the market starts acting funny. Sometimes, the tipoff will be what is called the "Professional Market" price pattern. This is a series of small volume, short thrust days curving over or under on a thin arc on the price chart. Count on this price pattern as a warning, and stand aside until you know for sure what the market is going to do. See June 81 Gold chart, Figure 63, for an example of the professional market price pattern.

4. *Common Bottoms and Tops*

   a. V bottoms or tops, see Mar. 83 Oat chart, Figure 64.
      Oats, Wheat and Pork Bellies are especially characterized by the V's in their price patterns. The thin markets are more apt to turn quickly, since there is a smaller following, but Wheat has always been a "V" bottom type even though it has large volume and open interest.

      Note what pattern is currently being exhibited by the chart patterns and expect this to continue.

   b. U bottoms.
      Gold, Stock Index futures and Corn are especially noted for "U" bottoms or tops. The U bottom is a lot like the "V" bottom, except is more rounded and consumes more time in turning. See the Oat chart for examples of this (Figure 64).

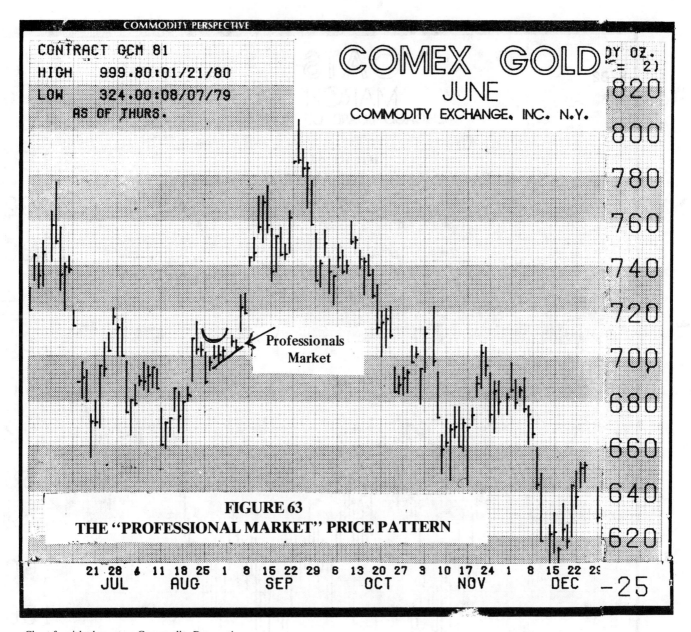

FIGURE 63
THE "PROFESSIONAL MARKET" PRICE PATTERN

Chart furnished courtesy Commodity Perspective

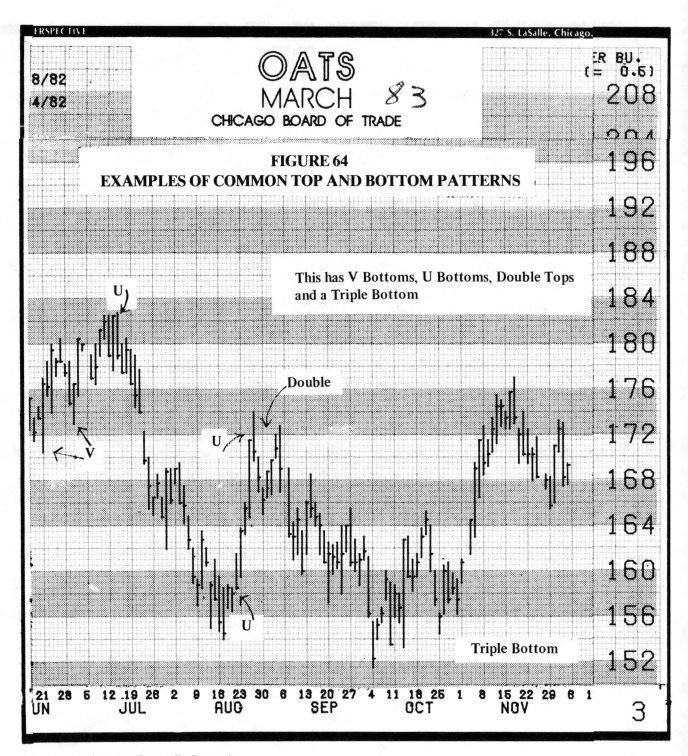

FIGURE 64
EXAMPLES OF COMMON TOP AND BOTTOM PATTERNS

This has V Bottoms, U Bottoms, Double Tops and a Triple Bottom

Chart furnished courtesy Commodity Perspective

c. Double or Triple bottoms or tops.

See the Mar. 83 Oat chart, Figure 64.

When not in a top or bottom price action, most commodities can be expected to have at least two, and usually three, spikes in congestions.

Double and triple bottoms are more often found in GNMA's, T-Bonds, and Beans. The Beans make these patterns differently, however. They tend to form triangles and wedges in their price patterns. These have the double and triple bottoms and tops, but this pattern is more bunched and sometimes on a skew to the rest of the price action. The spaces between the swings are wider than the regular double or triple bottom, too. See the Jan. 83 Soybean chart for examples of triangles and wedges (Figure 65).

d. Saucer bottoms.

Since cotton came back into competition with the synthetics due to the higher price of oil, we do not see many Saucer bottoms. The increases in the price of commodities due to inflation, and the increase in the volume of the futures markets has about eliminated Saucer bottoms.

e. The "Pole" pattern.

See Apr. 81 Live Hog chart, Figure 66, for examples.

This price pattern is expected in the middle levels of a campaign. It is typified by a run up or down of the market. Then the price charts make what resembles a flag or pennant that appears to be hanging on the pole. Markets like this are over-balanced in either supply or demand. The Flag or Pennant is merely a pause before the market goes back the way it came, especially if the flag part is small. Large swinging Flags or Pennants without long poles are not reliable. These may go either way.

While these are some of the more prominent characteristics of market action, I don't claim to have completely covered the subject. Each trader should know his markets for himself and make his own list of traits commonly exhibited by the price patterns.

VI.   RETRACEMENT SIZE EXPECTATIONS

The best help comes from knowing what is normal or abnormal in market action. This is covered in the Fibonacci section, but I'll summarize

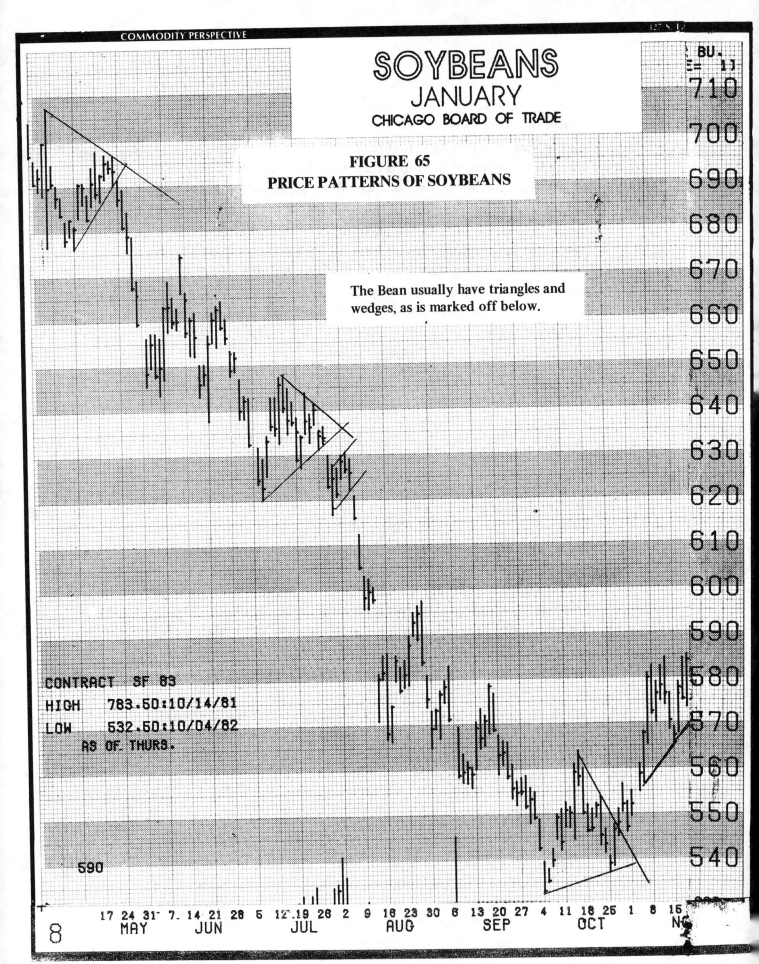

SOYBEANS
JANUARY
CHICAGO BOARD OF TRADE

FIGURE 65
PRICE PATTERNS OF SOYBEANS

The Bean usually have triangles and
wedges, as is marked off below.

CONTRACT SF 83
HIGH   783.50:10/14/81
LOW   532.50:10/04/82
    AS OF THURS.

590

17 24 31 7. 14 21 28 5 12.19 26 2 9 16 23 30 6 13 20 27 4 11 18 25 1 8 15
  MAY   JUN   JUL   AUG   SEP   OCT   N

8

Chart furnished courtesy Commodity Perspective

164

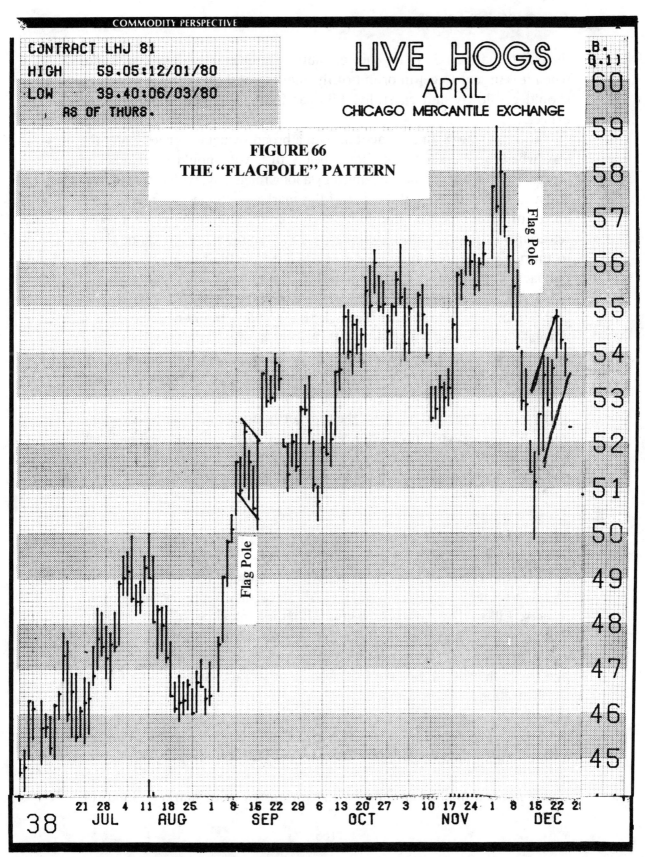

CONTRACT LHJ 81
HIGH   59.05:12/01/80
LOW   39.40:06/03/80
, AS OF THURS.

LIVE HOGS
APRIL
CHICAGO MERCANTILE EXCHANGE

LB.
(0.1)

FIGURE 66
THE "FLAGPOLE" PATTERN

Flag Pole

Flag Pole

38   21 28   4 11 18 25   1   8 15 22 29   6 13 20 27   3 10 17 24   1   8 15 22 28
         JUL   AUG   SEP   OCT   NOV   DEC

165

the points that pertain to urgency or caution in the market. There are times when it is urgent to get in or out of the market, and other times when one should go slowly and carefully. Fibonacci can help you know what to expect.

If there has been topping action, with a broad swinging congestion at the top, when the market breaks down below this, you should enter quickly; especially if the break is accompanied by a long range day, with large volume, and a close near the low of the day. If this market continues down on a steep angle of over seventy degrees, don't expect anywhere near a 60% retracement. In fact, do not expect even a 50% retracement. It will be closer to thirty-eight, if that much, according to how far the run goes before the pullback. The longer the run or leg, the less of a pullback you should expect.

Use the angle of travel to judge when to expect the forty, fifty, or sixty percent retracement. The sharper the angle, the less the amount of pullback you normally can expect. There should be at least a fifty-five degree angle in a down market, and a forty-five degree angle going up. So with the length of the previous leg and the steepness of the angle, along with the Fibonacci ratios, you should get a fairly close estimate of the action.

If you're in the third leg from the top, (or bottom) and if price is coming out of a congestion of only three weeks or less, then the fifty percent pullback is more normal. The last main thrust often reverses quickly, and has a sizeable pullback—much larger than those in the middle levels of price action.

VII.   WHAT ABOUT ELLIOTT?

The use of Elliott can help with this type of analysis. The best markets for Elliott are the Stock Indexes and Gold, since they represent millions of traders. Elliott Theory works better with these markets. Elliott used the Dow Jones Average, or some large average for most of his work.

The main place I recommend urgency with Elliott use is when a main 0-4 line has been crossed. See the 1983 Mar. Swiss Franc chart, Figure 67, for an illustration.

VIII.   LABELING PRICE REVERSAL PATTERNS

One needs a method of labeling the various types of markets, kinds of

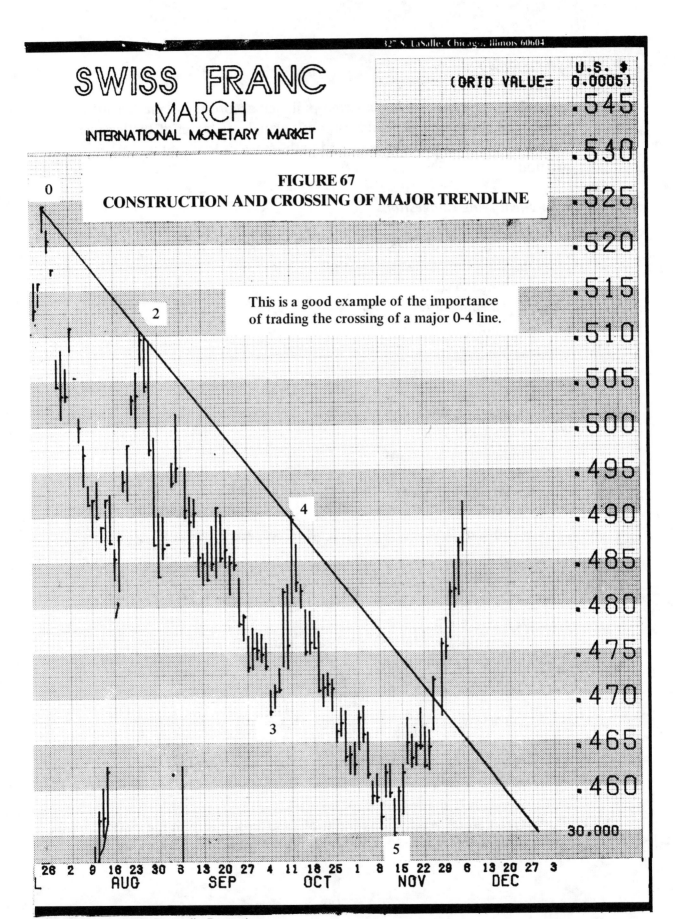

SWISS FRANC
MARCH
INTERNATIONAL MONETARY MARKET

(GRID VALUE= 0.0005)

U.S. $

FIGURE 67
CONSTRUCTION AND CROSSING OF MAJOR TRENDLINE

This is a good example of the importance
of trading the crossing of a major 0-4 line.

.545
.530
.525
.520
.515
.510
.505
.500
.495
.490
.485
.480
.475
.470
.465
.460

30,000

26 2   9 16 23 30   6 13 20 27   4 11 18 25   1   8 15 22 29   6 13 20 27   3
        AUG   SEP   OCT   NOV   DEC

167

congestions, and the typical expected pullback according to market price action. The pullback is dependent upon the angle of travel of the leg just before the pullback, and also is related to the stage or level of the market in question.

A. *Identifying Congestions*
 1. By Size
   a. Short and small (Short vertically and small horizontally)
   b. Short and large
   c. Tall and small
   d. Tall and large

 2. By Shape
   a. Triangle
   b. Flag or Pennant
   c. Irregular
   d. Flat and Wide
   e. Tall and Wide
   f. Labored moves are congestions going on an angle

B. *Identifying Pullbacks*
 1. By Size
   a. 40% to 50%
   b. 60% to 70%
   c. Retracement

 2. By Shape
   a. Congestion
   b. Triangle (See Jan. 83 Soybean Chart, Figure 65)
   c. Flag or Pennant
   d. Double or Triple Top or Bottom
   e. Labored move
   f. Fast swing

C. *Legend for Fast Identification*
 1. V = V Bottom or Top.
 2. U means U shaped turns of the market.
 3. C represents congestions and triple bottoms or tops in the market.
 4. A number followed by the word "days" describes how many days

are used for a break or to validate a turn in the price swing. If there are the words "5 days," this means that one must wait for a close above (or below) the highs (or lows) of the last five days.

5. VS is a "V" bottom or top with a short leg.
6. VL is a "V" bottom or top with a preceding long leg.
7. US is a short leg with a "U" type turn.
8. UL is a long leg with a "U" type turn.
9. CS is a congestion of a short span size.
10. CL is a long span size congestion, concerned only with the peak to low space of each congestion.

IX. RULE SPECIFICS

1. *For The Angle Amount*

It is important to stick to the recurring angle if one can be found, because this is the dominant factor in "angle of travel" trading. Many commodities will travel up or down on irregular swings. Do not be overly concerned about the overall angle of travel because the important thing is finding the recurring angle for the shorter middle size swings evolving around the long term angle of travel. Those individuals with enough money and the temperament for long term trading may use the long term angle of travel, as taught in the "True Trend" section. The average trader will find it better to play the shorter swings, where there is less chance of giving up good winnings if the short swing turns out to be a long one.

2. *For V, U, and C Tops or Bottoms*

a. V = A turn or pivot in the market formed in three days or less.
b. U = five days or less taken to make a turn.
c. C = anything more than five days needed or taken for making a turn in the market. This includes double bottoms or tops, as well as congestions or triple bottoms or tops.

The count only includes the days in the process of the changing. Those days extending out of the change are not counted.

3. *Length or Size of Swings*

(In the testing research the size dimensions will be labeled at the

(continued on page 171)

169

HAP PRICE REVERSAL CHART

Angle Of Travel	Runaway Type	Swinging With Long Legs	Choppy Short Legs With Congestions Close Together	Pullback Analysis
30°	VS = 3 days	VS = 3 days	VS = 3 days	three days
	VL = not enough data on this combination			no data
to	US = 5	US = Not Distinguishable	US = 3	four days
	UL = 5	UL = 5 days	UL = 3 days	no data
40°	CS = 7	CS = 8 days	CS = 7 days	nine days
	CL = 6	CL = 7	CL = 6	no data
40°	VS = 3	VS = 3	VS = 3	two days
	VL = 2	VL = 3	VL = 3	two days
to	US = 5	US = 5	US = 5	four days
	UL = 5	UL = 5	UL = 6	four days
60°	CS = 7	CS = 7	CS = 8	eight days
	CL = 9	CL = 8	CL = 9	seven days
60°	VS = 2 days	VS = 2 days	VS = 3 days	two days
	VL = 2	VL = 2	VL = 3	two days
to	US = 5	US = 5	US = 5	five days
	UL = 5	UL = 5	UL = 6	four days
80°	CS = 8	CS = 7	CS = 8	seven days
	CL = 7	CL = 8	CL = 9	ten days

On the "C's" above for congestions, remember that the measurement is for the span of the congestion, whereas the "V's" and "U's" are short or long according to whether or not the previous swing or leg is short or long.

To be of value I used current data but did not have a sufficient number of incidents for good averaging on some combinations. As time goes on I will obtain better results. Let this be a warning that each person needs to test this for himself, so he can know what to expect as an average number of days for making a turn with various sizes of legs going on various degrees of angle; and the number of days to expect in a pullback for each of these situations.

beginning of each test run. The following are some examples to show what to expect. Remember, the congestion is not concerned with the previous swing but measures the true range from peak to low within the actual congestion).

a. SWING SIZE IDENTIFICATION TABLE

	Long	Short
1. Wheat	25¢ or more	anything less
2. T-Bonds	3¢ or more	anything less
3. Gold	20.00 or more	anything less
4. Cotton	5¢ or more	anything less
5. Pork Bellies	5¢ or more	anything less

b. CONGESTION SIZE IDENTIFICATION TABLE

	Long	Short
1. Wheat	10¢	anything less
2. T-Bonds	3¢	anything less
3. Gold	10.00	anything less
4. Cotton	2¢	anything less
5. Pork Bellies	5¢	anything less

4. *Stages of the Market*

Since I used a computer for testing and analysis, I'm not including the levels of the market in the trading examples. The problem is telling a computer to go find the various levels of the market. If you want to devise a way to include this breakdown in your work, you may do so, but it is not included in our testing at this time. Bottoms and tops usually have more pronounced differences than the middle stages of the market.

Accumulation-distribution analysis work is discussed in my book, *"Eight New Commodity Technical Trading Methods."* This analysis is useful when a bottom or top is suspected, but so far has not been integrated into the "Fast or Slow" trading method. Read the comments in Section 3 above for points to keep in mind when you're actually trading.

5. *A Pivot or Turn of The Market*

A valid pivot is formed when there are at least two days of higher highs (that are higher by at least as much as the variance amount as given in the

171

table on pg. 181. This must be followed by two lower highs, that are lower by the variance amounts (as described above for the higher days).

The reverse of this will define a down pivot or turn. There must have been two lower lows (by the variance amount), followed by two days of higher lows of at least variance amount.

These turns are identified as high points (HIPS) for upturns and low points (LOPS) for downturns by some market analysts. This two-day-up and two-day-down definition sometimes occurs in a very small price range and will appear on the chart as merely a jiggle in the price movement.

X.   ANALYSIS RESULTS

A.   *The Swings Or Legs*

Surprisingly, the testing shows that "V" tops or bottoms are not affected much by the angle of travel, but there is more apt to be a two day "V" top or bottom if the swing or leg is longer.

There were practically no short-legged "U" shaped tops or bottoms. Here, again, it was surprising to find that the longer legged swings (going 60° or more) are more apt to have "U" shaped bottoms or tops.

B.   *The Congestions*

Large congestions are those that are taller (swinging in a larger span). There were many more congestions occurring in steep angles with fast momentum. These larger congestions were found mostly when preceded by long legs, as measured by the above swing size identification table.

In general, if a pullback is longer or larger than has been the previous usual condition, then look for a congestion or choppy market for the period following this pullback.

There are more apt to be congestions in the 60° to 80° angle category than in the less fast markets, especially if there has been a long swing.

Congestions are also found between short swings or in the middle areas of a trading range on the 30° to 60° *rate of acceleration. These congestions can often be used as measuring points for swing length estimations.*

C.   *Pullback Analysis*

  1. Short swings
      There is just as good a chance to have "V" tops or bottoms on

short swings as there is to have "U" tops or bottoms.

Most of the pullbacks on short swings are found in the faster markets, of 60° or more. This has been very revealing and points out common misconceptions often heard about the market action.

2. Long Swings

There are not apt to be pullbacks on long swings in the 30° to 40° category. Even with a 40° to 60° angle of travel there were very few pullbacks on long swings. Most of the pullbacks are found for the short "V's" and "U's," regardless of angle of travel. Long swings usually have their pullbacks in a shorter time period than found in the short swings (See Figure 63).

XI.   COMMODITY CHARACTERISTIC SUMMARY

I used Wheat, T-Bonds, Gold, Cotton, and Pork Bellies as representative of the various categories or types of commodities. For this study, I cannot go into detail on every commodity, but this study should teach you what to expect and how to go about the work necessary to pursue further analysis.

1.   *Wheat*

This commodity travels in legs having an angle of 60° or more, with swinging thrusts. You can conclude that any time it is not on this steep an angle there is a congestion.

Use a close beyond the last three closes as an entry signal. There would be few losses even in congestions and the added earnings will compensate for using a longer term entry signal.

Rules for trading will be given for each commodity. These rules were found to be best after a lot of testing. One should plan to keep optimizing on about three month intervals. As you read this, they will need updating again.

Preliminary testing summary sheets may be seen in the table labeled "Averages for Five Commodities" on the following page. I studied each commodity for the last three years and labeled all of the swings according to their length, kind of bottom or top, and number of days taken to make a turn. Then when all this was done I averaged each category. This work was

AVERAGES FOR FIVE COMMODITIES

	Angle	Category	Days Needed For Reversal
		VS	3
	30°	VL	0
I	to	US	5
	40°	UL	5
		CS	8
		CL	0
		VS	3 (2.52)
	40°	VL	2
II	to	US	4
	60°	UL	4
		CS	8
		CL	9
		VS	3 (2.55)
	60°	VL	2
III	to	US	5 (4.56)
	80°	UL	4
		CS	8 (7.5)
		CL	8

then used to set up conditions for change of trend, entry, exit, stops, and reentry. Each of these required a number of variations. Using only four for each, not counting the stops, there are sixteen different possibilities to check for each of the last three years.

2. *T-Bonds*

In 1980 the dominant angle was 60° or more. Trade on a close beyond the last three day's closes.

Things slowed down to a 45° angle in 1981 and 1982. There are also a lot more congestions in these two years. To avoid the congestions one would have to use a close beyond the last eight closes, but this would have given up a lot of money in the non-congestion areas.

Note the absence of travel on an angle of 40° or less. Even in the slower moving periods, if the Bonds did not swing on an angle of 40° or more there was a lot more congestion and choppy action.

3. *Gold*

For the last three years Gold has been swinging at a fast rate. Eighty degree angles are dominant.

There are three times more "V" bottoms than for other commodities, and three days is all that is necessary for turn requirements. More congestions are found after long swings.

4. *Cotton*

Traders who remember the Saucer bottoms may think of the "good old days." Now, with the higher price of oil, cotton has become very active again. One will find a lot of two day bottoms or tops—the other extreme from the old Saucer bottoms. Using a three day passing of previous closes (on close only) would be best for reentries.

There is no obvious number of days that can be used in place of a change of trend rule. Legs generally end with a congestion, especially if there has been a long swing.

Cotton has many small congestions and labored moves, even in markets that are trending. These Sideways movements are not so much pullbacks as they are a period of pausing in the market.

The dominant angle is seventy degrees.

5. *Pork Bellies*

Three day price reversals are dominant, along with a 70° angle of travel. These usually swing so much that a change of trend requirement will not increase profits. It is interesting to note that the Japanese Yen quite often travels a lot like the Bellies, so similar trading rules may be used for each.

After the Bellies go about twelve cents, expect a large congestion; or the market should go into a choppy eight cent up and down swing, resulting in a mostly sideways market for several weeks.

XII.   USING THE WEEKLY RULE

A lot of these price reversal patterns may be recognized by some as the use of the weekly rule altered according to the characteristics of a commodity, its stage of development in the market, and its angle of travel. Many investors use the weekly rule in their trading, but it is best not to pick some random number of days for reversals (when this number of days has its highs or lows overcome). The number of days should be related to the common characteristics of a market, according to its momentum of travel. Some commodities get killed using Donchian's twenty day reversal time period. The trader needs to study the commodity carefully to learn the most prevalent types of bottoms and pullbacks, and apply this to the momentum of the market.

Look at the Price Reversal chart on Page 170. The first type of market examined is the Runaway or fast moving market, with lots of momentum. This type of market should not normally be going less than sixty degrees on its angle of travel. Pullbacks of the first leg in a commodity having "V" bottoms or tops should not have more than a two day reversal. Congestions in the first leg should not have more than three days of continuous reversal on each swing of the legs in the congestion. Now go to each kind of market, with its type of bottom and degree of travel. You can see how the days should change according to the circumstances. When actually doing this, the degree of travel and the kind of bottom or top most common for the commodity to be traded are most vital. So when you see that a market is making a kind of bottom (such as the "V") then you would only apply this one kind in your trading, according to the angle of travel and the type of market. When it is shown by at least three months optimizing that a different type of market is prevailing, then change the numbers of days accordingly.

Note that you should expect quick reversals if there is steep fast action during bottoming.

The short leg swinger or choppy markets usually have their congestions in the middle of their swings, since this is the balance point of the whole swing.

XIII.   EXAMPLES OF WHEN TO TRADE

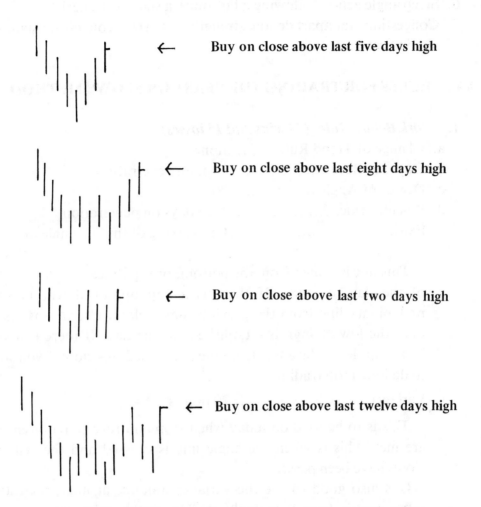

← **Buy on close above last five days high**

← **Buy on close above last eight days high**

← **Buy on close above last two days high**

← **Buy on close above last twelve days high**

Reversing these, or turning them over, would make sell signals.

XIV.   RULES ON URGENCY OR CAUTION IN TRADING

1. Anything not normal is a warning that needs special attention. Erratic action or Professional Arcs are examples.
2. Breakouts from lengthy congestions need quick action.
3. Price patterns that have been repeating require special attention, to judge if the time is right for another such move in the market.
4. A failure, or break, in the rhythm previously followed calls for a

change.
5. Long flagpole markets need a fast entry.
6. Steep angle action following a bottom is a sign of strength.
7. Congestions far apart denote strength. A narrow congestion span size also indicates strength.

XV.   RULES FOR TRADING THE "FAST OR SLOW" METHOD

1. ***Pork Bellies Rules (45 wins and 15 losses)***
   a. Change of Trend Rule..........none
   b. Days for Reversal...............two, on penetration
   c. Degree of Angle to use.........70°
   d. Re-entry rule....................Two days on penetration
   e. Exit...............................On crossing of the 70° angle line

   This line is drawn from the bottom, or top if heading downward, of the day of entry. If there is a gap up, or down, make a preliminary line from the previous day's close. Use this as a stop until the low or high is established for the day. If there is a very large gap, leave the angle from the previous day's close if you want to do long term trading.

   f. Variance.........................20 points

   This is to be used on a day when stop and reverse requirements are met. This is when the angle line is crossed and the last two closes have been passed.

   It is also good to use the variance amount at line penetration (after profits have been built up) for traders using long term or "Slow" type trading. This is because the low or high for a day will often go to the seventy degree angle line, barely penetrate it, then proceed on for more nice profits. The seventy degree line drawn from the high, low, or previous day's close is one of the best support or resistance lines for trading.

   g. If the market gaps on the open by at least twice the amount of the variance (40 points) and does not come back to fill this gap from the previous day's close, then draw the 70° line from the previous day's close for use as the exit line.

   h. Stand aside when price is near a previous high, low or gap, until it is passed.

178

2.   *Rules For Trading Japanese Yen*
      (Same rules as Pork Bellies except Variance is 10 points)

   1. Wins = 44
   2. Losses = 16
   3. Even = 13
   4. If gaps open the amount of twice the variance (20 points) and trading does not come back to fill this gap, then draw the 70° angle line off of the previous day's close.
   5. Wait for previous pivots or gaps to be passed before trading (if they are close by).

3.   *T-Bond Trading Rules (69 wins - 33 losses - 17 even)*

There is no trend reversal rule necessary. The best angle found is seventy degrees. Enter on penetration of the last three closes, and re-enter on penetration of the last three closes. Exit on penetration of the last three closes. The exit is either/or, meaning it can be penetration beyond the last three closes, or crossing the seventy degree line, whichever comes first. The variance amount is eight points.

If price gaps away from the previous close on a trade entry signal, and if the gap is at least twice the amount of the variance, use the previous close from which to draw the line. If the low for the day of entry is twice the variance amount (or more) below the previous day's low on a buy signal day, then use the previous day's low for the seventy degree line. On a sell signal day, if the high is twice the variance amount above the previous day's high, then use the previous day's high for drawing the seventy degree line. When using the close to draw the line, it should start from the outer edge (close to the next day's line) on the cross bar showing where the close existed.

Stand aside on trades near the previous high, low, or gap until they are passed.

4.   *Rules For Trading Wheat*

   1. Enter on a penetration beyond two closes.
   2. Exit on a penetration of the last two closes.
   3. Re-enter on penetration of the last two closes.
   4. Stop and reverse (SAR) if the last two closes were penetrated at the time of exit.
   4. Use a 70° angle line from the low or high when a trade is made.

179

5. ***Wheat Rules (A Second Set) - (34 wins and 25 losses)***

I. Change of Trend Rule (labeled CTR), is on a close beyond the last eleven closes. Trade on the close on the twelfth day.

II. The angle from the low (or high) of the day of entry is 70°. If a gap makes the low (or high) unfeasible (more than 2 cents in grains), use the previous day's close until a low or high is established on the trade day. If the day of trade is a long range (having the low beyond the average range for the last ten days) below the previous day's low, then use the previous day's low instead of the low for the day of the trade.

III. Exit when the 70° line is crossed.

IV. Re-enter when there is a close beyond the last three closes, if there has not been a change of trend. The change of trend must never be traded against.

V. If trading is close to a previous high, low, or gap, wait until it is passed.

6. ***Rules For Trading Cotton***

1. Enter after penetration of the last two closes.
2. Exit on 70° angle line.
3. Re-enter if the last two closes are passed.
4. Stop and Reverse (SAR) if the last two closes cross beyond the line.
5. "CL" means "cover loss" and "CW" means "cover win."

7. ***Rules For Trading Gold (98 wins - 41 losses)***

1. Enter when price goes below (or above) the last two closes on penetration.
2. Exit on the 80° angle line. Draw the angle from the high (or low if downward) of the day of entry. If it is a case where there is a far-distance-opening, use the previous day's high (or low) until the day of entry is over, then make a new angle from the high (or low) of the day of entry.
3. Variance is $2.00.
4. Re-enter on penetration of the last two closes.
5. Do not enter a second trade (or use data for the second trade) until the current trade is finished.
6. Do not trade until previous pivots or gaps are passed.

FIGURE 68
COMMODITY VARIANCE AMOUNTS TABLE

Symbol	Name	Exch.	Units	Size	CF	$/Pt.	K	Var. Pts.	Input	Min TIC	Point Value
M	GNMA CDR Certificate	CBT	$/32	$100,000	-2	31.25	32	8	0.25	1 Pt. = 1/32%	1/32%
TR	Treasury Bonds	CBT	$/32	$100,000	-2	31.25	32	8	0.25	1 Pt. = 1/32%	1/32%
MC	C. D. GNMA	CBT	$/32	$100,000	-2	31.25	32	8	0.25	1 Pt. = 1/32%	1/32%
C	Corn	CBT	¢/BU	5,000 BU	-1	50.00	1	8	1.0	2 Pt. = 2/8¢	1/8¢
O	Oats	CBT	¢/BU	5,000 BU	-1	50.00	1	16	2.0	2 Pt. = 2/8¢	1/8¢
S	Soybeans	CBT	¢/BU	5,000 BU	-1	50.00	1	16	2.0	2 Pt. = 2/8¢	1/8¢
W	Wheat	CBT	¢/BU	5,000 BU	-1	50.00	1	16	2.0	2 Pt. = 2/8¢	1/8¢
CO	Cocoa	NYCE	$/TN	10 MET TON	Ø	10.00	1	10	10.0	1 Pt. = $1.00	$1.00
PL	Platinum	NYME	$/OZ	50 T. OZ	1	0.50	100	40	0.4	10 Pt. = $ .10	$ .01
PW	Plywood	CBT	$/M SQ FT	76032 SQ FT	1	0.76032	100	100	1.0	10 Pt. = $ .10	$ .01
SV	Silver	COMEX	¢/OZ	5,000 T. OZ	1	0.50	100	10	0.1	10 Pt. = .10¢	.01¢
SI	Silver	CME	¢/OZ	5,000 T. OZ	1	0.50	100	10	0.1	10 Pt. = .10¢	.01¢
LB	Lumber	CME	$/M B D FT	130,000 B D FT	1	1.30	100	100	1.0	10 Pt. = $ .10	$ .01
GC	Gold	COMEX	$/OZ	100 T. OZ	1	1.00	100	200	2.00	10 Pt. = $ .10	$ .01
SM	Soybean Meal	CBT	$/TON	100 TON	1	1.00	100	100	1.00	10 Pt. = $ .10	$ .01
DM	Deutschemark	IMM	$/DM	125,000 DM	4	12.50	10^4	10	0.1	1 Pt. = .01$	.01$
SF	Swiss Franc	IMM	$/SF	125,000 SF	4	12.50	10^4	10	0.1	1 Pt. = .01$	.01$
BP	British Pound	IMM	$/L	25,000 L	4	2.50	10^4	10	0.1	5 Pt. = .05$	.01$
CD	Canadian Dollar	IMM	$/CD	100,000 CD	4	10.00	10^4	10	0.1	1 Pt. = .01$	.01$
JY	Japanese Yen	IMM	¢/Y	12500 M Y	4	12.50	10^4	10	0.1	1 Pt. = .01¢	.01¢

Chapter Twelve

It Pays To Be Different

WHAT ARE MEDIAN LINES?

These are lines from a pivot through the middle of the next swing, extending out so that price may intercept them. Dr. A. H. Andrews of FFES conceived this market tool as a quick and easy way to apply W. D. Gann's angle method. Median Lines are at least 60% accurate in finding the pivots of a market. I showed traders how to make and use these in the book *"Eight New Commodity Technical Trading Methods."* Anyone who does not know how to use them should learn. For the many who do understand and appreciate the Median Lines, I have good news. There are some very helpful differences and innovations from the old Median Line technique that should improve profits from the market.

REVERSE MEDIAN

The first different Median Line is the Reverse Median Line. This goes from the middle of a swing to the next pivot, extending out where price may contact it (see Figure 70). Dr. Andrews mentioned this very briefly in some old work. I did a lot of testing with Reverse Median Lines and found them to be helpful. I taught a little about these Reverse Median Lines in *"Eight New Commodity Technical Trading Methods,"* also.

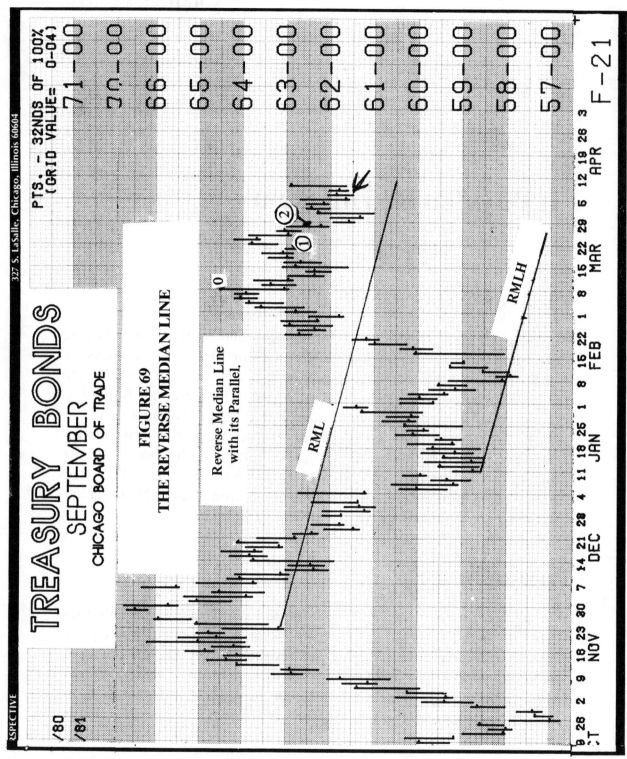

These RML's as they are called, are especially good in choppy markets, whereas the regular ML's are better in zigzag swinging markets. The RML's will give the trader information earlier than the regular ML's that are to be drawn. At times, the RML turns into a median line, becoming a multi-indicator line, (MIL). These MIL's are stronger and better indicators. This knowledge can often make the difference in being in on the right side of the market for a trade.

SECOND SWING MEDIAN LINES

A trick not known by many traders is to skip the first swing's middle and go on to the second swing's middle, extending this line out to hit price action (See Figure 71).

This works better from a distant pivot while in a fast running market. In consolidation periods, these do not work often. The overall percent of these being right is not as good as the regular median lines, unless you know when to use them. First, here is how *not* to use them.

WHEN NOT TO USE SWML'S

1. As I mentioned earlier, these do not work well in congestions or consolidation areas.

2. Elliott Flat areas or Triangles are other places where they do not usually work.

WHEN TO USE THE SWML'S

1. Anytime the regular ML does not have price action in a position to reach the reglar ML, try using the SWML. This will often find the end of a swing movement.

2. Use them in fast runs; especially a small reaction in a fast run. If you want to estimate where the rally or reaction will end, but the regular ML line looks much too far away to intercept price, then go to the SWML and this should help.

185

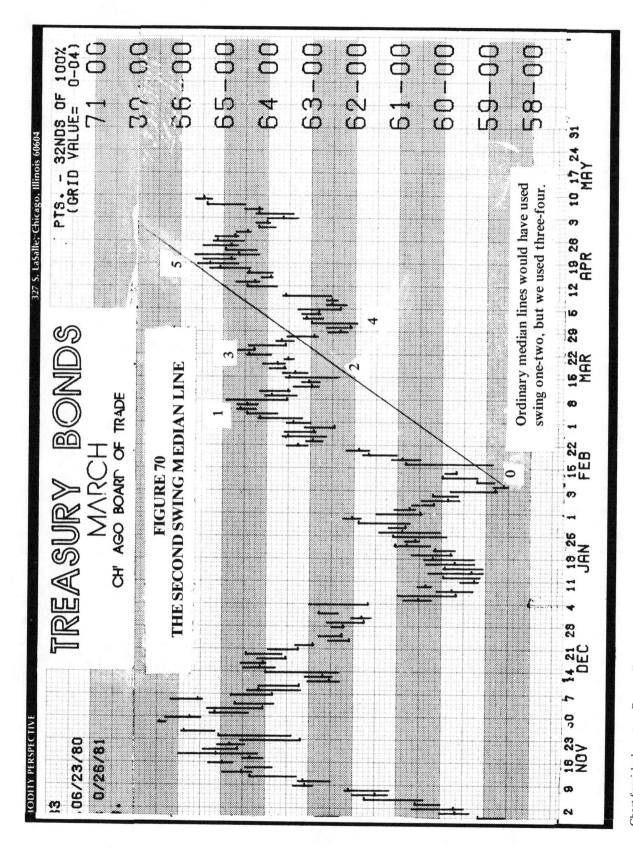

TREASURY BONDS
MARCH
CH' AGO BOARD OF TRADE

FIGURE 70
THE SECOND SWING MEDIAN LINE

Ordinary median lines would have used swing one-two, but we used three-four.

PTS. - 32NDS OF 100%
(GRID VALUE= 0-04)

Chart furnished courtesy Commodity Perspective

THE SECOND MEDIAN LINE (See Figure 72)

If the regular ML has been overshot by price movement, then go to the first previous median line and extend this on down (or up) to see if it will be in line for interception. You are simply using the previous ML rather than the current one.

Use these when there has been a lot of fast action in the market. FFES teaches the use of parallel lines to the ML drawn from the pivots of the swing being bisected. These are called MLH's. Price will often pass through these lines parallel to the median lines. When this happens, the FFES instructions are to draw another line out the same distance away from the parallel as the parallel was from the median line, and call this the warning line. I have not found these too effective, however. It is better to use an older median line that extends to the current price action. Knowing to do this will sometimes make the difference in how well you do in the market.

USING THE 0-2 LINE WITH ML'S

You can get advance warning as to whether or not a median line will be good by using the 0-2 lines. This is a line drawn on the tips of any two pivots and its parallel going from the middle pivot (see Figure 73). 0-2 lines can be one of the most valuable aids when trading with median lines.

THREE WAYS THEY CAN HELP YOUR TRADING

1. If price does not reach the parallel to the 0-2 line, you know that the movement is weak.
2. If it shoots past the line with ease, you know the market is strong.
3. Many times there are places where one cannot draw median lines that are relevant to current price action on a short term basis, but you can make a 0-2 line with its parallel (this makes up for the "V" bottoms or tops). Other times you'll find that a median line is just not applicable. This will make a lot of difference in your trading, as you now know some of the tricks of the trade. You are able to know the direction of the market when the median lines are not available to help.

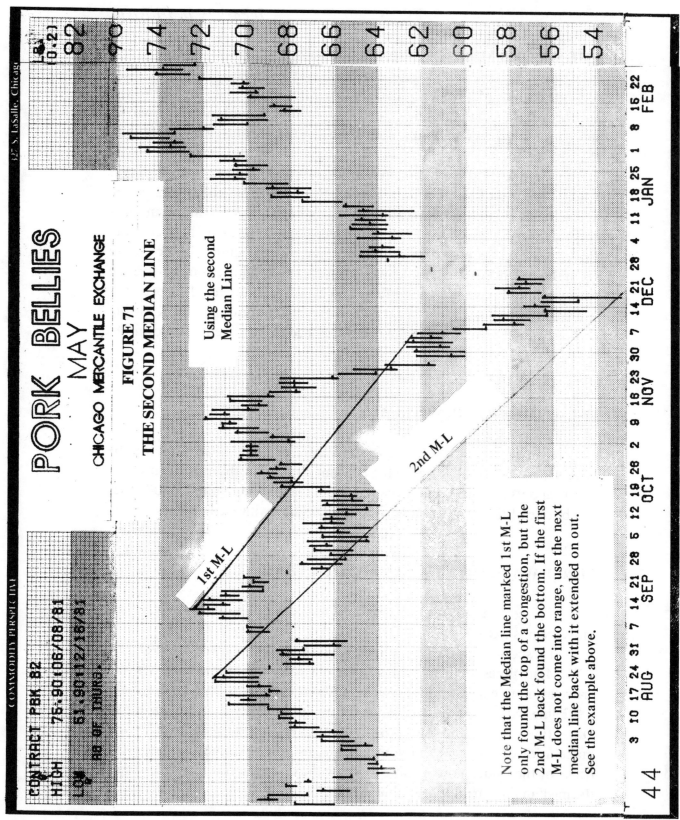

PORK BELLIES
MAY
CHICAGO MERCANTILE EXCHANGE

FIGURE 71
THE SECOND MEDIAN LINE

Using the second
Median Line

2nd M-L

1st M-L

Note that the Median line marked 1st M-L
only found the top of a congestion, but the
2nd M-L back found the bottom. If the first
M-L does not come into range, use the next
median line back with it extended on out.
See the example above.

CONTRACT PBK 82
HIGH 76.90 06/08/81
LOW 51.90 12/16/81

Chart furnished courtesy Commodity Perspective

188

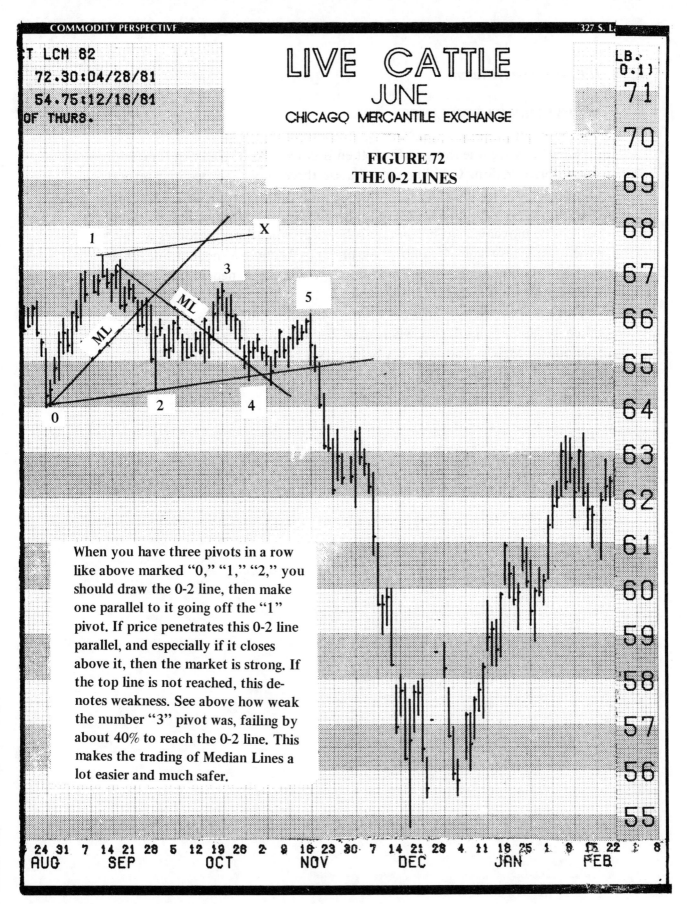

T LCM 82
72.30:04/28/81
54.75:12/16/81
OF THURS.

LB.
0.1)

LIVE CATTLE
JUNE
CHICAGO MERCANTILE EXCHANGE

FIGURE 72
THE 0-2 LINES

When you have three pivots in a row like above marked "0," "1," "2," you should draw the 0-2 line, then make one parallel to it going off the "1" pivot. If price penetrates this 0-2 line parallel, and especially if it closes above it, then the market is strong. If the top line is not reached, this denotes weakness. See above how weak the number "3" pivot was, failing by about 40% to reach the 0-2 line. This makes the trading of Median Lines a lot easier and much safer.

Chart furnished courtesy Commodity Perspective

189

MULTI-INDICATOR LINES

Some lines are one thing at first, then become another later in time with future price action. One line can change three times, to become several different types of indicators. These are called Multi-Indicator Lines, or MIL's. This is very interesting to watch develop. A straight line converts with price movement to become another type, then later becomes a third type of indicator line. A multi-pivot line may become a median line, then perhaps a balance point line. Trend lines often become median lines, and 0-2 lines sometimes turn into median lines.

These multi-indicator lines are usually stronger than others. They have a much better win/loss ratio when used for trading. It pays to be on the lookout for MIL's. They are very helpful (see Figures 74 through 77).

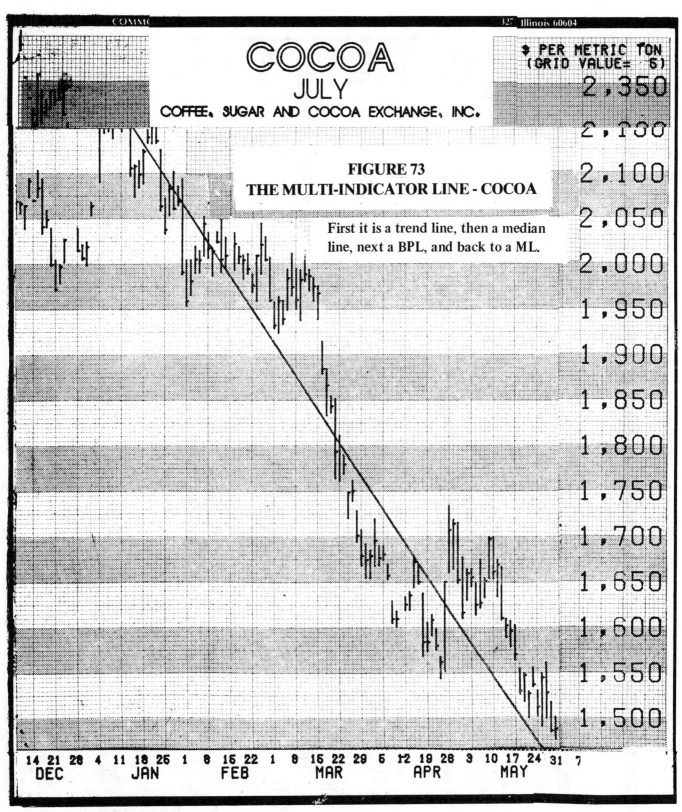

COCOA
JULY
COFFEE, SUGAR AND COCOA EXCHANGE, INC.

$ PER METRIC TON
(GRID VALUE= 5)

FIGURE 73
THE MULTI-INDICATOR LINE - COCOA

First it is a trend line, then a median
line, next a BPL, and back to a ML.

Chart furnished courtesy Commodity Perspective

GINNIE MAE
SEPTEMBER
CHICAGO BOARD OF TRADE

FIGURE 74
THE MULTI-INDICATOR LINE - GINNIE MAE

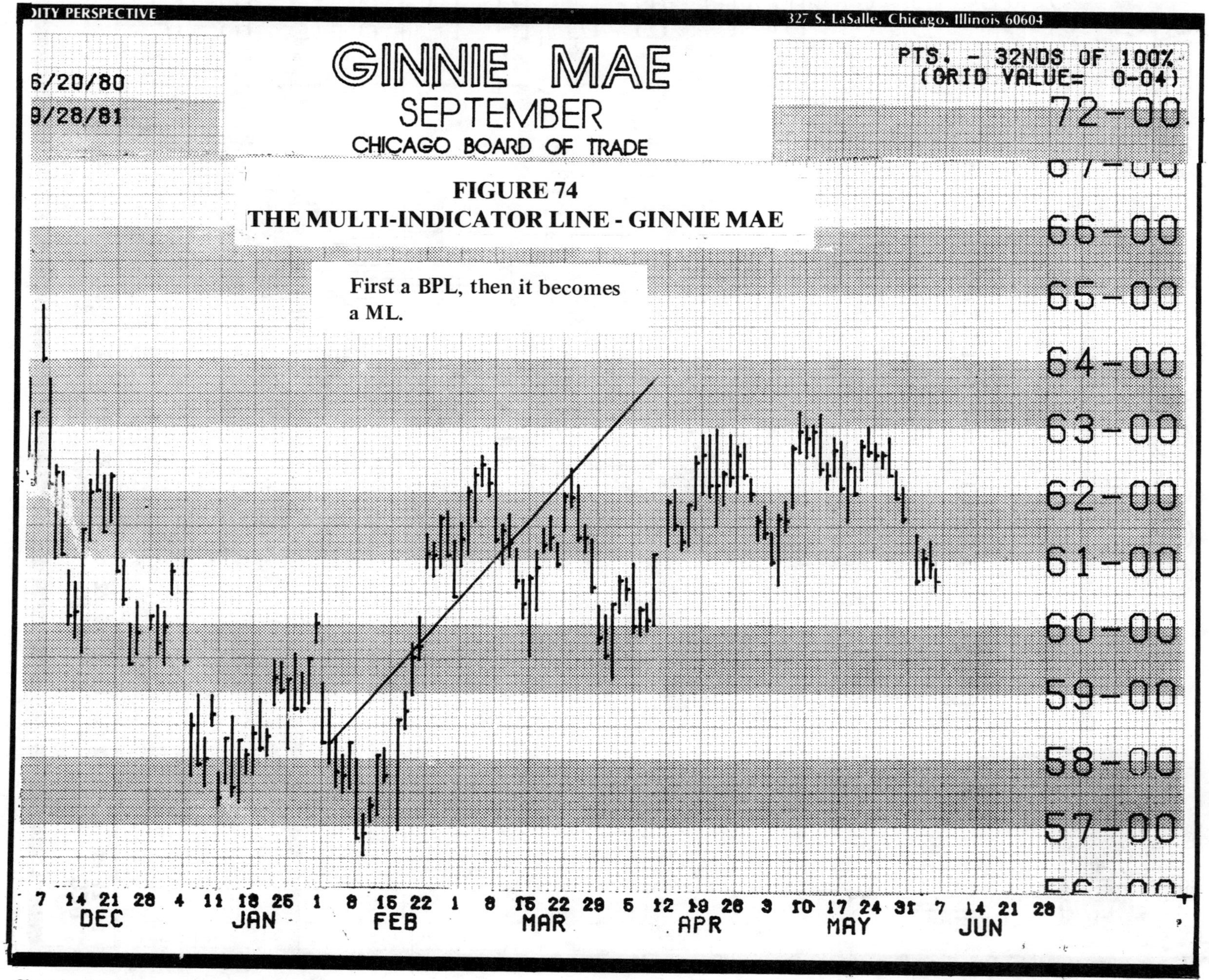

First a BPL, then it becomes a ML.

PTS. - 32NDS OF 100%
(GRID VALUE= 0-04)

192

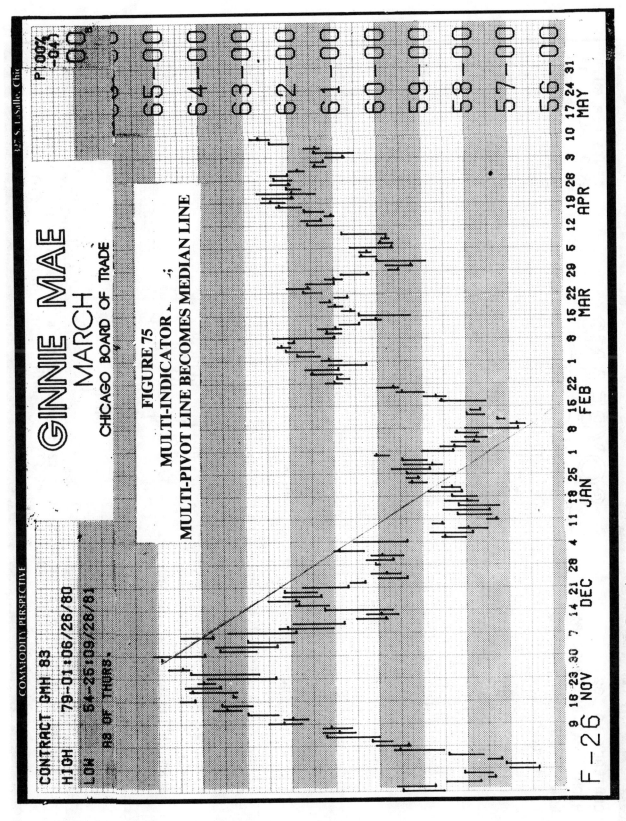

COMMODITY PERSPECTIVE

GINNIE MAE
MARCH
CHICAGO BOARD OF TRADE

CONTRACT GMH 83
HIGH 79-01:06/26/80
LOW 54-25:09/28/81

FIGURE 75
MULTI-INDICATOR
MULTI-PIVOT LINE BECOMES MEDIAN LINE

F-26

193

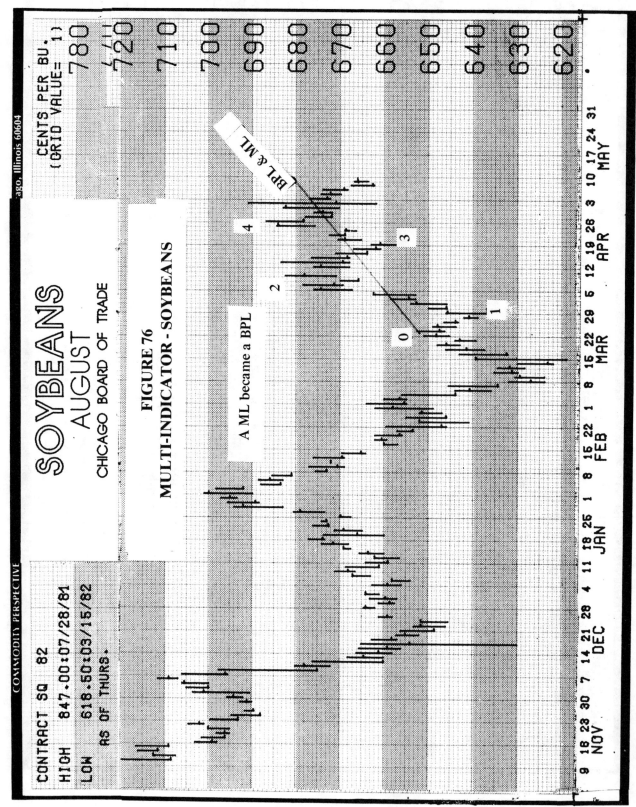

FIGURE 76

MULTI-INDICATOR - SOYBEANS

A ML became a BPL

BPL & ML

194

Chapter Thirteen

Long Term Trading

I. WHY THIS IS DIFFERENT

If someone is trading one hundred contracts in commodities expecting to keep them for a year, he should have special techniques. In this case, technical work may not be enough. These big traders always spend a lot of time and money on the fundamentals of the commodity itself. In fact, most are producers or heavy users of the commodity and know the supply and demand picture from first hand experience. It's facetious to imply they can be taught about their own business. Where they want help is in weather predicting and in forecasting of the economic conditions. For weather predicting, they use a good meteorologist and for the economics they try to get advice from those having a good reputation in this type of work. Weather predicting and economy predicting both have about the same kind of results. They are often wrong!

On the week of July 5, 1982, twelve of the nations's leading economists were quoted in the Wall Street Journal, all predicting higher interest rates. I told some friends at that time rates would come down, and they did. With these kinds of results, one may wonder why anyone would try to invest a million dollars or more in the market, thinking he can predict how things are going to be a year later. Just the supply and demand side of the predicting is hard for some. But everyone knows that even a supply or demand shortage or abundance will not offset a failing economy very long.

195

Many businesses have lobbyists and friends in Washington trying to obtain inside information on what to expect.

II. GOVERNMENT TAMPERING

Ever since the depression, starting in 1929, the government has been trying more and more to control the economy. Much of this is due to pressure from people who want someone to take their risks or assume their obligations. There are laws now affecting nearly every phase of our lives, and government watchdogs around trying to enforce these laws. It would be nice to always have a big brother protect us from our bad conditions; but so far, it hasn't been that easy for most people.

It has been proven many times that individuals cannot corner a market for very long, but government meddling can certainly change things so a business will lose money. Good businessmen keep up with events in Washington that affect them. This part is not too difficult, because the government issues a lot of information. The hard part is knowing whether or not the government is contracting the economy or expanding it. This is the job of the Federal Reserve Board, which tries to be free from political influence. But sometimes it is very hard to tell what kind of policy is being advocated by the Feds.

III. WHAT USED TO WORK

A few years ago, one only had to watch the Federal Discount Rates, the money supply, the monetary base, and the velocity of money; but, since 1981, things have changed.

It is evident to most people that buying a lot of speculative material hoping to make money in a contracting economy will take special funding and someone who really knows what he is doing. Long term traders must be able to foresee or know when the government is going to be restrictive or supportive, and the Feds do not announce this in plain language. It takes special knowledge of the causes and effects of the conditions involved. Here is a summary of the factors that are important.

1. High Federal Fund and Federal Discount Rates means restriction and

deflation.

2. An increasing money supply and monetary base means expansion and inflation by the government.

3. Slow business activity with curtailed sales and restrictions on exports means recession and perhaps a depression.

4. Higher prices mean lower profits and less income to pay workers. The ratio of money made to money invested affects employment.

5. Commodities will not go up in price over a sustained period of time if the money supply and monetary base are going down, along with a decline in the velocity of money. The long term trader must be able to tell when there is an expansionist or contracting policy in play by the government.

IV. WHAT IS DIFFERENT NOW

The thing that has caused things to be different is the excessive borrowing of the government to pay for the enormous National Debt. The government formerly contracted debts, then inflated the economy to pay off these debts. Now things have gotten top heavy. We are approaching a condition where those who work and produce are not able to provide enough taxes or revenue for the government to meet their needs. If companies do not have enough left for themselves to make a profit, they usually close shop. We are in danger of having a depression along with super inflation.

Pumping billions of dollars into the economy trying to prop things up does not help if the profit incentive is too low. Many people do better not working.

This is why the old economic indicators have quit working. The long term traders need to learn these differences to overcome their problems.

V. FACTS WE MUST FACE

1. Business is not going to increase or continue if there are no profits.

2. Borrowing of money is necessary at a rate where profits can be made.

3. If the government borrows most of the available money, this puts business in a bind.

197

4. Debasing our money with inflationary practices cannot continue forever. Eventually, someone has to pay with something of real value.

5. Businessmen who are successful adjust to these conditions and do what is necessary to preserve their capital, hoping for another chance in another time or place.

6. Long term speculators cannot make money in a flat market, like that in most of 1977. The market must be moving either up or down.

VI.   WHEN NOT TO TRADE

The long term speculator must sit out the dormant transitionary periods, or learn to trade short term. Here are some things to help you know when not to trade long term.

1. If there is confusion and uncertainty about government policies, expect interest rates to churn around, along with money supply figures and other economic indicators.

2. Flat velocity of money or money multiplier lines on the graph imply that nothing is going to move until this changes.

3. Businessmen do not risk their personal wealth, as a rule. They borrow money for expansion in a corporation, and let the corporation go broke if they fail. Until money is available at a rate where it can be borrowed and still make a profit, those who have money keep it and cut back to stay even in their business. The long term trader can expect deflationary conditions when interest rates are high. If the interest rates get too high, this is a time to be on the short side, mostly.

VII.   WHAT CAN BE RECOMMENDED

1. As Gann said. "If in doubt, stay out." Do not put on a long term position until you are sure about the money policy of the government.

2. Watch real money supply. Real money supply is the percent of change of the Consumer Price Index, subtracted from the percent of change of money supply. If real money has not been moving up or down much, then the economy is in a stalemate.

3. Compare real money supply with the change in industrial activity or

sales. If this, too, is flat, then the odds are slim for long term trading.

4. You seldom make money in the market until you have conditions favorable. There are times when you make more by sitting on the sidelines.

5. After 1939, there was a long term bull market, with the contraction periods shorter than the expansion periods. But now, it may be the other way around. Look for longer contractions and shorter expansions for several years to come.

6. Do not take anyone's word or recommendation. Know for yourself what is happening and what are your chances of winning.

7. If you do not understand the basics of this type of trading analysis, get some good books, like David Rhoad's *"How to Survive a Spastic Economy,"* published by J. D. Press, P. O. Box 22674, San Diego, CA 92122.

8. Long term indicators like the True Trend Lines, Gravity Center Lines, and Thrust Lines are good and will help tremendously; but for the trader of large positions to do better he should properly analyze the prevailing economic conditions.

(See Figure 77 through 83 for examples of charts issued by the Federal Reserve Board).

FIGURE 77
MI MONEY SUPPLY - FED. RES. BOARD

MONEY STOCK (MI)
AVERAGES OF DAILY FIGURES
SEASONALLY ADJUSTED

1982	BILLIONS
JUL. 28	451.3
AUG. 4	453.5
11	453.6
18	454.9
25	456.2
SEP. 1	457.1

LATEST DATA PLOTTED WEEK ENDING: SEPTEMBER 1, 1982

CURRENT DATA APPEAR IN THE BOARD OF GOVERNORS' H.6 RELEASE.

MI CONSISTS OF CURRENCY HELD BY THE NONBANK PUBLIC PLUS COMMERCIAL BANK DEMAND DEPOSITS
HELD BY THE NONBANK PUBLIC (EXCLUDING THOSE HELD BY FOREIGN BANKS AND OFFICIAL INSTITUTIONS)
AND OTHER CHECKABLE DEPOSITS OF ALL DEPOSITORY INSTITUTIONS PLUS TRAVELERS' CHECKS

MONEY STOCK (MI)

COMPOUNDED ANNUAL RATES OF CHANGE, AVERAGE OF FOUR WEEKS ENDING:

TO THE AVERAGE OF FOUR WEEKS ENDING:	9/2/81	12/2/81	2/3/82	3/3/82	3/31/82	4/28/82	6/2/82	6/30/82
2/ 3/82	10.3							
3/ 3/82	7.7	10.0						
3/31/82	6.8	7.8	-2.2					
4/28/82	7.8	9.3	3.5	8.3				
6/ 2/82	6.7	7.3	2.2	4.6	6.2			
6/30/82	5.6	5.6	0.8	2.3	2.7	-2.7		
8/ 4/82	5.3	5.2	1.2	2.4	2.7	-0.7	-0.6	
9/ 1/82	5.7	5.8	2.5	3.7	4.2	1.8	2.9	6.4

PREPARED BY FEDERAL RESERVE BANK OF ST. LOUIS

200

FIGURE 78

ADJUSTED MONETARY BASE - FED. RES. BOARD

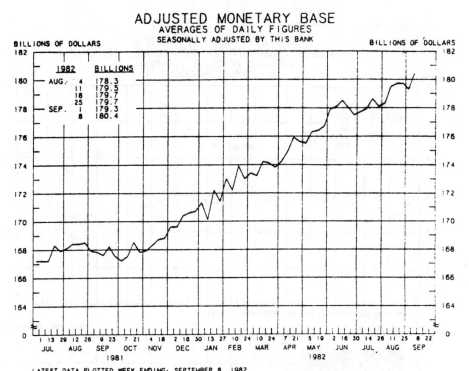

ADJUSTED MONETARY BASE
AVERAGES OF DAILY FIGURES
SEASONALLY ADJUSTED BY THIS BANK

1982	BILLIONS
AUG. 4	178.3
11	179.5
18	179.7
25	179.7
SEP. 1	179.3
8	180.4

LATEST DATA PLOTTED WEEK ENDING: SEPTEMBER 8, 1982

THE ADJUSTED MONETARY BASE CONSISTS OF: (1) RESERVE ACCOUNTS OF FINANCIAL INSTITUTIONS AT FEDERAL RESERVE BANKS, (2) CURRENCY IN CIRCULATION (CURRENCY HELD BY THE PUBLIC AND IN THE VAULTS OF ALL DEPOSITORY INSTITUTIONS), AND (3) AN ADJUSTMENT FOR RESERVE REQUIREMENT RATIO CHANGES. THE MAJOR SOURCE OF THE ADJUSTED MONETARY BASE IS FEDERAL RESERVE CREDIT. DATA ARE COMPUTED BY THIS BANK. A DETAILED DESCRIPTION OF THE ADJUSTED MONETARY BASE IS AVAILABLE FROM THIS BANK.

ADJUSTED MONETARY BASE

COMPOUNDED ANNUAL RATES OF CHANGE, AVERAGE OF FOUR WEEKS ENDING:

TO THE AVERAGE OF FOUR WEEKS ENDING:	9/9/81	12/9/81	2/10/82	3/10/82	4/7/82	5/5/82	6/9/82	7/7/82
2/10/82	5.7							
3/10/82	6.3	10.3						
4/ 7/82	6.2	9.1	7.4					
5/ 5/82	6.7	9.5	8.6	8.1				
6/ 9/82	7.3	9.8	9.3	9.3	11.1			
7/ 7/82	7.0	9.1	8.4	8.2	9.0	8.2		
8/11/82	6.7	8.4	7.6	7.2	7.7	6.7	4.3	
9/ 8/82	6.9	8.4	7.8	7.5	7.9	7.2	5.8	6.3

PREPARED BY FEDERAL RESERVE BANK OF ST. LOUIS

201

FIGURE 79

MONEY MULTIPLIER - FED. RES. BOARD

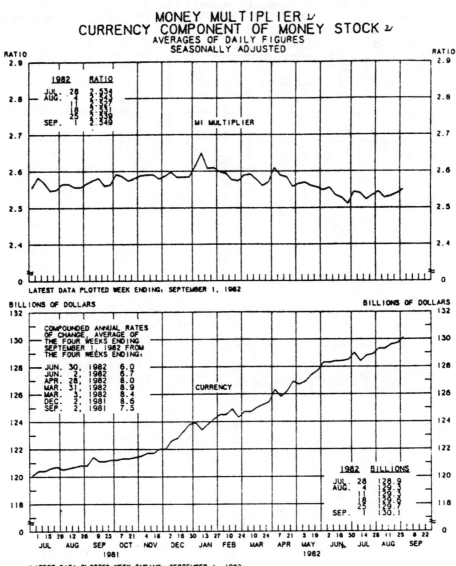

MONEY MULTIPLIER 1/
CURRENCY COMPONENT OF MONEY STOCK 2/
AVERAGES OF DAILY FIGURES
SEASONALLY ADJUSTED

LATEST DATA PLOTTED WEEK ENDING: SEPTEMBER 1, 1982

1/ RATIO OF MONEY STOCK (M1) TO ADJUSTED MONETARY BASE

2/ CURRENT DATA APPEAR IN THE BOARD OF GOVERNORS' H.6 RELEASE.

PREPARED BY FEDERAL RESERVE BANK OF ST. LOUIS

FIGURE 80
INTEREST RATES - FED. RES. BOARD

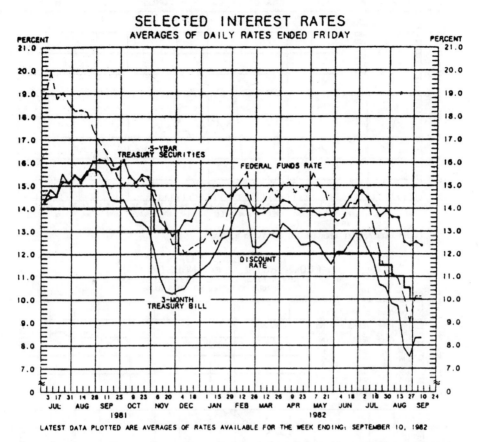

SELECTED INTEREST RATES
AVERAGES OF DAILY RATES ENDED FRIDAY

LATEST DATA PLOTTED ARE AVERAGES OF RATES AVAILABLE FOR THE WEEK ENDING: SEPTEMBER 10, 1982

1982	FEDERAL FUNDS ▦▦	3-MONTH TREASURY BILL	6-MONTH TREASURY BILL ▦▦▦	1-YEAR TREASURY BILL	5-YEAR TREASURY SECURITIES	LONG-TERM TREASURY SECURITIES
JULY 2	14.81	12.81	13.42	12.86	14.73 ▵	13.85
9	14.47	12.23	12.98	12.50	14.48 ▵	13.68
16	13.18	11.71	11.97	12.06	14.10	13.40
23	12.14	10.64	11.44	11.29	13.66	13.11
30	11.02	10.51	11.38	11.50	13.89	13.30
AUG. 6	11.15	9.80	10.67	11.13	13.62	13.08
13	10.90	9.70	10.94	11.06	13.59	13.02
20	10.11	7.88	9.82	9.71	12.53	12.17
27	9.04	7.50	8.99	9.68	12.38	12.04
SEP. 3	10.15	8.31	9.75	10.12	12.54	12.16
10 ▦	10.14	8.32	9.61	10.04	12.38	11.97
17						
24						

▦ AVERAGES OF RATES AVAILABLE.
▦▦ SEVEN-DAY AVERAGES FOR WEEK ENDING WEDNESDAY TWO DAYS EARLIER THAN DATE SHOWN.
CURRENT DATA APPEAR IN THE BOARD OF GOVERNORS' H.15 RELEASE.
▦▦▦ NEW ISSUE RATE
RATES ON LONG-TERM TREASURY SECURITIES ARE COMPUTED BY THE FEDERAL RESERVE BANK OF ST. LOUIS.
TREASURY BILL YIELDS ON DISCOUNT BASIS.

PREPARED BY FEDERAL RESERVE BANK OF ST. LOUIS

FIGURE 81

BORROWING FROM FEDERAL RESERVE BANKS - FED. RES. BOARD

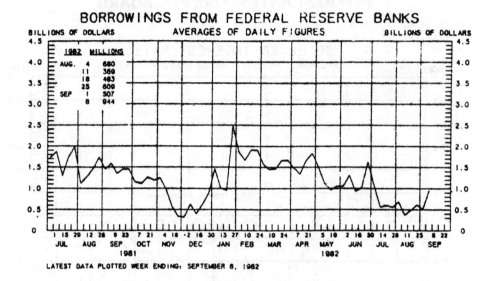

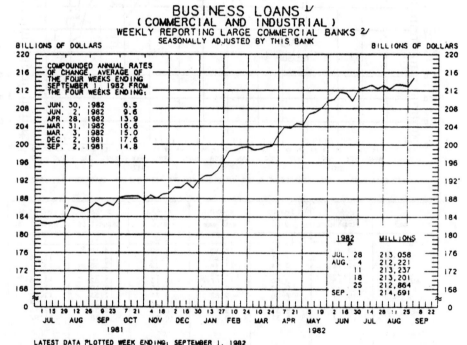

The information and data in these charts may be obtained free by writing to: Federal Reserve Bank of St. Louis, P. O. Box 442, St. Louis, Missouri 63166. Ask for: "U. S. Financial Data"

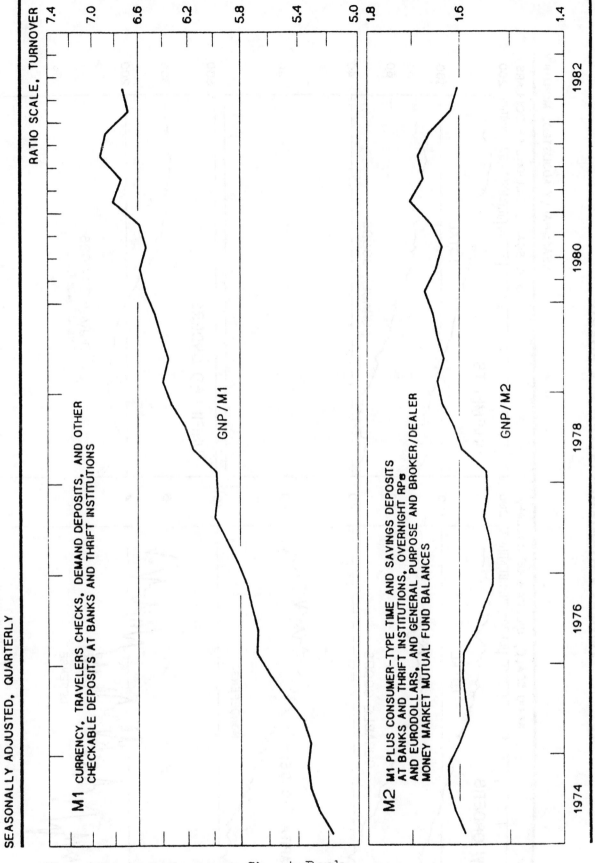

FIGURE 82

INCOME VELOCITY OF MONEY - FED. RES. BOARD

SEASONALLY ADJUSTED, QUARTERLY

RATIO SCALE, TURNOVER

M1 CURRENCY, TRAVELERS CHECKS, DEMAND DEPOSITS, AND OTHER CHECKABLE DEPOSITS AT BANKS AND THRIFT INSTITUTIONS

GNP / M1

M2 M1 PLUS CONSUMER-TYPE TIME AND SAVINGS DEPOSITS AT BANKS AND THRIFT INSTITUTIONS, OVERNIGHT RPs AND EURODOLLARS, AND GENERAL PURPOSE AND BROKER/DEALER MONEY MARKET MUTUAL FUND BALANCES

GNP / M2

Federal Reserve Chart Book
Board of Governors of the Federal Reserve System
Publications Services, MP-510
Washington, D.C. 20551   Cost $7.00 a year

FIGURE 83
ORDERS AND SHIPMENTS - FED. RES. BOARD

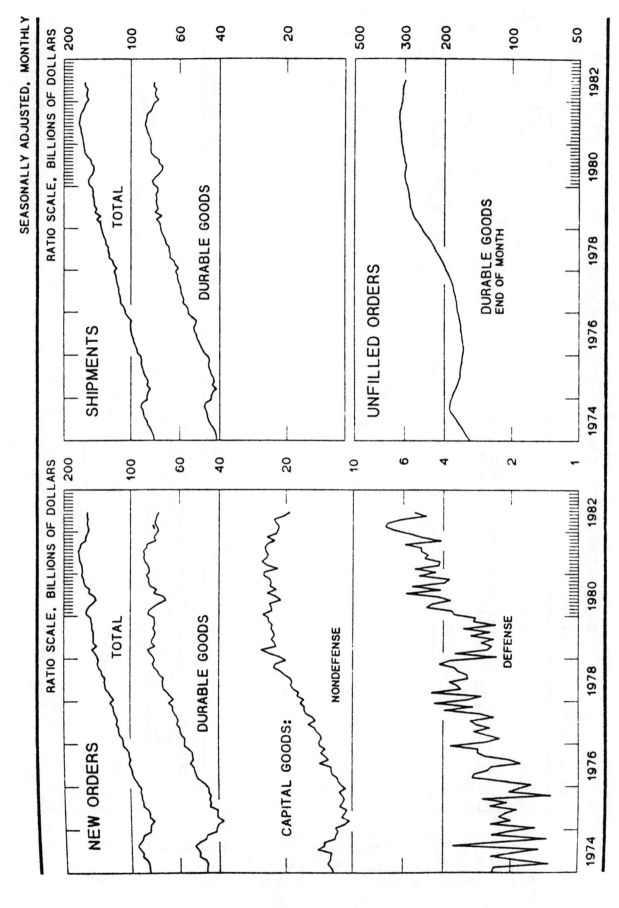

206